The Believable Futures of American Protestantism

Essays by

Thomas Sieger Derr
James Davison Hunter
Thomas C. Oden
Timothy L. Smith

and
The Story of an Encounter by
Paul T. Stallsworth

Edited and with a Foreword by
Richard John Neuhaus

WILLIAM B. EERDMANS PUBLISHING COMPANY
GRAND RAPIDS, MICHIGAN

Published by Wm. B. Eerdmans Publishing Co.
in cooperation with
The Rockford Institute Center on Religion & Society

Copyright © 1988 by Wm. B. Eerdmans Publishing Co.
255 Jefferson Ave. S.E., Grand Rapids, Mich. 49503

Library of Congress Cataloging-in-Publication Data:

The Believable futures of American Protestantism
essays by Thomas Sieger Derr . . . [et al.] ; and The story of an
encounter by Paul T. Stallsworth ; edited and with a foreword by
Richard John Neuhaus.
      p.   cm.   (Encounter series ; 7)
  "Published . . . in cooperation with the Rockford Institute Center on
Religion & Society"—T.p. verso.
  Based on a conference sponsored by the Rockford Institute Center on
Religion & Society.
  ISBN 0-8028-0207-9
  1. Protestant churches—United States—Congresses.
2. Protestantism—Congresses.   I. Derr, Thomas Sieger, 1931-
II. Neuhaus, Richard John.   III. Center on Religion & Society (New
York, N.Y.)   IV. Series: Encounter series (Grand Rapids, Mich.) ; 7.
BR515.B514 1988
280'.4'0973—dc 19   88-3722
                                               CIP

Contents

Foreword

Not many years ago there was a storm of public controversy over the emergence of what came to be called the Religious New Right. "What's the fuss about?" responded Jerry Falwell and others. "The liberals have been mixing religion and politics for years and years. We're just following their example and have the same freedom to press a political agenda that they have always claimed." Now, more jaded readers might find confirmation of their hunch that in time everything repeats itself, whether as tragedy, farce, or just confusion. For instance, here is a 1987 item from *United Church News*, a publication of the United Church of Christ, in which the Rev. Richard Hughes is responding to criticism that the UCC is too political: "I don't see anyone criticizing Jerry Falwell or Pat Robertson for their brand of political religion. So why not give the rest of us the same freedom?" Historians of American religion may note that this may be the first instance of what was once the mainline and is now commonly called the "oldline" invoking the precedent of the new mainline in order to justify its participation in public life.

Reinhold Niebuhr comes in for extensive attention in the pages that follow. Niebuhr, of course, was famous for his appreciation of irony in American history and world affairs. There is also dramatic and sometimes whimsical irony in the affairs of American religion. It seems doubtful in the extreme that the mix of people, traditions, and concerns involved in this book could have been assembled forty or even ten years ago. The book comes out of a conference called to consider "the believable futures of American Protestantism." Yet the title itself is filled with ambiguities. Believable is not the same thing as desirable. And just what is meant by American Protestantism? Large parts of Lutheranism and Anglicanism have been nervous about being included in the category "Protestant," although both traditions have contributed powerfully to what it means to be Protestant. And the sectors of religion that are, as it were, feeling their oats in America today are by no means satisfied with designating themselves Protestant. They are, rather, evangelical, fundamentalist, or Pentecostal. So who is left to be more or less unambiguously Protestant? The answer would seem to bring us back to the mainline or the oldline or, less kindly, the sideline churches.

When we started planning this conference, our working title was "The Believable Futures of Mainline Protestantism." The planning group included Dean Kelley of the National Council of Churches, James Hunter of the University of Virginia, Elliott Wright of the National Conference of Christians and Jews, Paul Stallsworth of the Center on Religion & Society, and myself. In other words, it was emphatically a group of mainline Protestants. Why then did we drop the word *mainline* from the title? There was within this group and far beyond it an awareness that the mainline had in recent years come upon hard times. And perhaps it was not just a matter of recent years, since signs of the collapse of the religio-cultural dominance of the mainline were evident enough by the third decade of this century. To have a conference focusing exclusively on the mainline would run the risk of turning it into yet another postmortem on what went wrong. And, frankly, it might have invited the kind of "mainline bashing" in which some seem to delight. That might have been fun for a few, but it wouldn't have added much to our understanding. Another reason for dropping "mainline" from the title is that it really is true that no part of the religious reality can be understood apart from the whole. That may sound like a truism, but that is because it is true. For this reason the reader will notice that Roman Catholic participation and concern very much entered into the deliberations recounted here.

All that said, however, the book is very largely about the mainline. Timothy Smith puts our thinking into a framework reaching over a time when American Protestantism, then simply called evangelical Christianity, seemed more secure and less problematic. James Hunter sets the stage sociologically for the continuing drama that this book analyzes, noting the sundry ways in which what was once secure has become so maddeningly problematic. Thomas Derr makes a vigorous case for the ongoing imperatives that have shaped mainline (sometimes called ecumenical) Christianity, and the conference concludes with Thomas Oden's compelling appeal for the reappropriation of the Great Tradition. As you will read in the "Story of an Encounter," there was at moments during these days a sense that something very important was aborning. There was self-deprecating talk about a "new Reformation" or a "rebirth of neo-orthodoxy," but the talk was not entirely self-deprecating. Maybe something really new is afoot, some participants urged, and it should not be belittled. The Holy Spirit has worked through less likely means, it was suggested. I do not know if this sense of something portentous happening should be attributed to keen perception or unseemly pretention. All these factors and others were no doubt in play.

But it would be an injustice to the event, to the participants and, who knows, to the workings of the Spirit were I to downplay the palpable sense of excitement that marked this conference. I hope something of that comes through in the chapters that follow and in the "Story of an Encounter." There are here no triumphalist illusions about a mainline Protestant retrieval of its culturally dominant role. Rather, especially in the discussion of Thomas Oden's essay, there is an awareness of the need for repentance and, yes, of return to the theological truth claims by which the church is constituted. Apart from that constituting truth, all the historical and sociological concerns about religion and the formation of culture are trivial or even idolatrous. So do we end up calling this neo-neo-orthodoxy? That would be both clumsy and misleading. I think the conference did end on the note of the need to try to do what neo-orthodoxy attempted in the 1930s, but in a situation significantly different a half century later. Better stated, I take the concluding note to be that in our time, as in all times of the church's pilgrimage, the only future that can be both believed and desired is one in which Christian people attend more assiduously to that which makes them the church. The proper word for that is *orthodoxy*.

My special thanks to Robert Lynn of the Lilly Endowment, which funded the conference; to William Eerdmans, publisher and friend; to my colleague Allan Carlson of the Rockford Institute; and to Davida Goldman and Paul Stallsworth of the Center staff for good counsel, ready support, and the skills to see such an event through from conception to catering.

Richard John Neuhaus

THE ROCKFORD INSTITUTE
CENTER ON RELIGION & SOCIETY
NEW YORK CITY

Evangelical Christianity and American Culture

Timothy L. Smith

The dissolution of religious consensus in twentieth-century America, not only within the major religious traditions but in the external relations of each to the others, tends to distort our vision of the nation's religious history. The more extreme parties of Protestant modernists, whom secular scholars feel most comfortable with, and the most combative party of evangelicals, the fundamentalists, flourish by persuading academia and the news media that theirs is the only game in town. Middle-class black evangelicals stand aloof from black Pentecostals, and both groups reject the radicalism of Christian black nationalists. The vast majority of Roman Catholics, like the majority of white Protestants, stand midway between extremist camps, yet both insiders and outsiders are coming to see Catholics as divided into parties of modernists, social activists, charismatics, and reactionaries. Meanwhile, the world honors an activist and deeply spiritual pope who seems to fit into none of these parties and to embrace some of the most starkly competing ideals of each one. Jewish religious differences, of course, have been muted in this century by the strength of their united opposition to anti-Semitism, by their substitution of the language of ethnicity for that of religious faith, and by support of the state of Israel and its ethic of national survival. The result is to obscure the religious history both of the Jews who settled in this country before 1881 and of the vast company whose migration from Central and Eastern Europe began that year. Likewise, Eastern Orthodox Christians, whose numerous ethnic segments were able in the late nineteenth century to think of themselves as adjusting to life in the United States and Canada on the same religious terms, have in this century faced repeated challenges to their ancient commitment to ecumenical ideals. The flight after World War I of anti-Bolshevik White Russians and after World

War II of Orthodox refugees from Central and Eastern Europe included many who had been in business or the professions and a few who had owned large estates. Unlike the peasant migrants of earlier decades, the new exiles were inclined to embrace reactionary political and social policies as the only proper Christian response to the threat of communism, whether in Europe or America.

The consequence of this widespread breakdown of consensus has been the growing public and scholarly illusion that American society has been secularized—this despite the verifiable fact of an extensive revival of personal commitment in every North American religious tradition, including those that originated in Islamic or in Oriental Hindu and Buddhist cultures. That illusion is, I think, socially and politically unproductive. The prompting it gives to both political and religious obscurantism and the dissension it breeds over what Americans once thought were shared moral standards seem to me too great a price for either the United States or Canada to pay.

In the hope, therefore, of lighting up pathways that could lead us to a renewed though perhaps more modest consensus, I wish to lay out here a straightforward history of the relationship of evangelical Christianity to the shaping of American culture and to underline those aspects of the story that contributed to the moral and political consensus that my colleague John Higham has called "pluralistic unity," or "integrative pluralism." The conviction of our diverse oneness held this nation together in the nineteenth century, despite a bitter sectional conflict; and it helped to make our experiment in government of, by, and for the people a beacon of hope to almost the entire world.

Let me begin by stating what I imagine to be a rigorously historical definition of Protestant evangelicalism that seems generally acceptable to all these competing religious groups and yet admits of no easy compromises among them. I and my younger colleagues have employed it with increasing satisfaction in the analyses of twelve North American evangelical "movements" that we have made for the essays in our forthcoming book *The American Evangelical Mosaic*.

Both the term *evangelical* and its historical definition first became widely popular in England and America during the religious revivals of the eighteenth century associated with John Wesley's Methodist Arminianism, with George Whitefield's and William Tennant's Puritan Calvinism, and with the worldwide mission movement stemming from German Reformed and Lutheran Pietism. Though in Germany and elsewhere on the Continent the term *evan-*

gelical was unsatisfactory because it had previously been used to denote Lutheran as distinct from Reformed Protestants, contemporaries understood Pietism, particularly in its more aggressive Moravian expression, to be part and parcel of the developments that Britons and Americans called evangelical.

In all of these movements, thoroughgoing commitment to the authority of the Old and New Testaments, and hence to careful study of them, was both the basis of moral and spiritual revival and a chief means of spreading it. This had been true of Protestantism from the beginning, especially of the radical Mennonites, Brethren, and Quakers. These "peace churches" slowly identified themselves as a fourth evangelical movement. They shared with the others the conviction that the Hebrew and Christian Scriptures were permeated with the promise of a personal experience of salvation from sin, received in a moment of living faith, that Jesus called being "born again." Finally, all four of these inwardly diverse movements found that both the Scriptures and this inward experience of love for God and one's neighbor impelled them to missionary evangelism. These three characteristics—commitment to scriptural authority, the experience of regeneration or "new life in Christ," and the passion for evangelism—have marked evangelicals ever since. They were distinguishing marks not only in the four parent movements but also in the parties of evangelicals that emerged in the older state churches and in new movements that sprang up along their edges through the course of the nineteenth and early twentieth centuries.

RELIGIOUS PLURALISM

The larger impact of evangelicalism on American culture will be clearer, I think, if we begin by stressing its original pluralistic character. In our day, the notion prevails that pluralism in societies that were or are predominantly Protestant has been forced on a recalcitrant and usually Anglo-Saxon majority by mass Catholic and Jewish immigration, especially in the growing cities that were the centers of rapid cultural change. And modern students generally assume that pluralism led directly to a secularization of the culture. I do not wish to challenge such truth as may lie in either of those assumptions; I simply want to stress that the evangelical situation itself generated and circumscribed the force of pluralism. Understanding that fact might help contending parties in our present conflicted situation to search more hopefully for a consensus about morals rooted honestly in today's interfaith diversity.

Let me ask you where we should begin the study of North America's religious history in order to lay bare the roots of our twentieth-century situation. Certainly not, I think, either with the landing of William Bradford's tiny company of separatists at Plymouth in 1620 or with John Winthrop's great migration of Puritans to Charlestown and Boston in 1629. No colonial city was more unlike modern American cities than seventeenth-century Boston, where Cottons and Mathers dominated the religious scene. And claims that the less religious Chesapeake society of Virginia and Maryland was modern America in embryo are even less persuasive. Save for their English and Protestant character, neither of these points much more clearly to the modern situation than the establishment of New France. We should begin rather with the middle colonies, from Long Island Sound southward, paying attention to Maryland only at the end of the colonial period, when Baltimore's ties to an increasingly diverse backcountry made it over into the religiously plural and ethnically diverse community that Dutch-English New York and English-German Philadelphia had been for a hundred years. These three cities remain to this day classic models of North America's religious pluralism.

Colonial Philadelphia displayed with special clarity evangelical Protestant pluralism. William Penn not only welcomed to his new commonwealth his fellow Quakers—English, Welsh, Irish, and Dutch—but Rhineland German pacifists from both Mennonite-Anabaptist and radical Pietist circles. Poor Englishmen of Anglican and Puritan backgrounds soon began following the Quakers, as did Scottish and Scotch-Irish Presbyterians, in whose homelands evangelical beliefs and attitudes were spreading rapidly. Presbyterians in the Delaware and Susquehanna valleys soon were experiencing the religious awakenings that William Tennant and his sons initiated and George Whitefield brought to white heat. Calvinists, however, were not Christian pacifists. Neither were the poor Germans of various Lutheran and Reformed backgrounds who arrived in Philadelphia a generation after the peace people. The missionary pastors that these poor settlers were able to secure, after a number of years during which congregations of lay persons operated without benefit of clergy, were the Pietists Henry M. Muhlenberg and Michael Schlatter. These two soon came to be revered as founders of the Pennsylvania German Lutheran and Reformed communions, chiefly because they were able to persuade other young Pietist ministers to come over to America to help shepherd their "lost" countrymen. The result, of course, was the transformation of their congregations into evangelical communities.

Baptists came to the Delaware Valley a bit later in the century.

Sufficient numbers of English Baptists settled in and around Philadelphia to make the area the first heartland of the American Baptist movement. The city itself was the home of the Baptist Missionary Convention until the slavery controversy disrupted the denomination's unity. John Wesley did not send over Methodist preachers until the decade preceding the Revolutionary War. They found that the poorer families of English people who had filtered into New York City, Philadelphia, Wilmington, and Baltimore were a ripe field for the Wesleyan harvest, whether or not they had been faithful Anglicans in Great Britain. And so were the Anglical yeomen of Maryland, Delaware, and Virginia.

The adoption of the Quaker-Anabaptist idea of the separation of church and state by New York Presbyterian William R. Livingston and a growing number of the city's Anglicans and Dutch Reformed stemmed directly not only from the fact of religious pluralism but also from its evangelical character. The conservative parties of Anglicans and Dutch Reformed who opposed pluralism were both antidemocratic and suspicious of evangelical fervor.

The myth of a steep decline of religious commitment in revolutionary New York turns out to rest on the writings of conservatives who wished to perpetuate the remains of a religious and social establishment as a counterweight to the republican tendencies of evangelical culture. The New York missionary society, founded in 1795 on the model of one organized shortly before by diverse dissenters in London, anticipated the formation of the Connecticut missionary society by several years. The multiplication of local revivals throughout the United States and English Canada that are sometimes called (I think incorrectly) the second Great Awakening did not begin either at Yale College or at Cane Ridge, Kentucky, as variously argued in the past. They originated rather in the concerted effort and the growing sense of unity among evangelical pastors and congregations in New York City, Long Island, and northeastern New Jersey. Evangelicals in that region, as in the Delaware and Susquehanna valleys and the Maryland and Virginia backcountry, had become used to the idea that Christians could secure order and sustain moral behavior in a religiously plural republic by bringing the unchurched into a biblical experience of moral transformation. Whatever modern social scientists have made of the emergence thereafter of what they are pleased to call "civil religion," the ruling religious and moral ideas that pervaded the intellectual, economic, and political culture of the United States and Canada in the nineteenth century were grounded in biblical faith, defined evangelically and experienced personally.

It is not surprising, therefore, that new evangelical movements added during that century to the American Protestant kaleidoscope fit readily into both the evangelical moral consensus and the social and political order the consensus sustained. Consider, for example, the movement in which one might expect to find an exception to this rule—the increasingly segregated black Methodists and Baptists. Separate congregations emerged first in the mid-Atlantic cities and then, while troubled slaveholders were developing more stringent codes of both legal and social oppression, in the urban South. Black Christians demanded, first within the white churches and then in their own separate ones, a full measure of both the liberties and the moral and political responsibilities that other evangelicals enjoyed in a pluralistic nation. They read the Bible from the point of view of the oppressed, to be sure, and doing so nurtured a different sensibility. But in historical perspective, black Methodist and Baptist cultures were simply more intensely evangelical than their white counterparts with respect to Scripture, spiritual experience, and evangelism. This is evident in the fervent music, prayer, and preaching of their worship on the one hand and also in the moral insight of their lay and ministerial leaders. Black preachers dreamed more powerfully than white preachers of a kingdom of God in which unrighteousness (meaning, biblically, injustice) would be banished from the nation by the spread of saving grace.

The evangelical character of other new Protestant movements of the nineteenth century seems also obvious. Alexander Campbell's Disciples of Christ sought from 1809 onward to unite all true Christians on a platform that renounced "human" creeds in favor of Scripture alone. They saw in the Bible, of course, the same call to repentance and saving faith that others had seen, and the same obligation to soul-winning. Despite his irenic evangelism, however, Campbell became instead the founder of a New Testament sect. Its adherents, now numbering in three great aggregations possibly as many as six million persons, affirmed both Jacksonian democratic ideals and the separation of church and state, because they believed that the conversion of individuals is the only way to bring on the millennial dawn. The Adventist movement, which took shape a bit later among those who were shattered when the Second Coming of Christ did not take place in 1843-44, fits the same pattern. So do other more radical millenarian movements such as the Mormons and the Jehovah's Witnesses, whose evolving self-definition moved them away from not only a Protestant but a Christian identity. The unique early teachings of Joseph Smith stem from his reaction not so much against the evangelical style of religious belief and ethical behavior as against what the young prophet believed were the contradictions in doctrine, ethics, and expectations of the future the Bible had allowed diverse Protestant movements to embrace. *The Book of Mormon* and a large portion of Smith's subsequent revelations that now constitute the *Doctrine and Covenants* of the Church of Jesus Christ of the Latter-day Saints proclaim a Christian faith that became complete and coherent only when a new volume of sacred writings had reconciled old theological conflicts and charted the history and the future of that faith in the New World.

I must cut short here this account of evangelical diversity in the United States and Canada. It moves on to the emergence during the last half of the nineteenth century of ethnic Protestant evangelical denominations (such as the Missouri Synod of Lutherans, mostly German, and the Christian Reformed Church, mostly Dutch) and of the Wesleyan holiness movement. Three new movements of the twentieth century stand in the same religious lineage—the fundamentalists and the two communities of Pentecostals, one white and the other black.

But I must underscore the self-conscious character of the evangelical embrace of the cultural and political implications of Protestant pluralism. By the middle of the nineteenth century, leaders of all these movements affirmed that biblical religion would flourish best under the separation of church and state and that only such a religion could generate both the moral sensibility and the social idealism that were necessary to sustain a modern republic. Viewed against the broad sweep of Christian history since the Reformation, this was an immense achievement, though not one we would expect to find Jewish and Catholic leaders of that era applauding. Nevertheless, I think both the formal structure and the social tendencies of that pluralism were parents to the interfaith idealism that Americans in the United States and Canada have struggled throughout the twentieth century to incorporate into law and custom.

A BIBLICAL CULTURE

The extent to which explicit reference to biblical teachings characterized every aspect of American culture was sometimes a surprise to Europeans who traveled here during the middle decades of the nineteenth century. Nowadays, however, scholars specializing in many aspects of our nation's history have found it commonplace. Why did respect for the Hebrew and Christian Scriptures become so important to nineteenth-century Americans? Certainly the task of forming a nation among people of diverse ethnic, political, and religious backgrounds required an authority that transcended tradition. The founding generation made a sharp break with old customs of aristocracy, royal authority, and class prerogative, appealing not only to reason and common sense but to scriptural teaching. Moreover, they regarded a democratic republic boasting freedom of religion as a perilous experiment. The selfish passions of competing groups and classes would tear it apart unless all could willingly submit to ethical principles that transcended particular religious traditions. The Bible set forth those principles, as even such Deists as Thomas Jefferson and Benjamin Franklin affirmed and rationalists like Thomas Paine could not deny. But what could secure the willing submission of self-interested citizens to it?

The principal evangelical contribution to making the Hebrew and Christian Scriptures the living constitution undergirding the document forged at Philadelphia and adopted by popular vote was the religious experience of saving faith, empowering human beings, as the epistle to the Romans puts it, to fulfill the righteousness of the law. In the formation and structure of their congregations, in the exposition of Christian ethics and theology, and in their successive revolts from both ecclesiastical and political authority, Puritans, Presbyterians and Pietists, Methodists, Baptists, and Mennonites had appealed to Moses and the prophets, to Christ and the apostles. Now, in the shaping of what they prayed would be a Christian republic, they relied on the moral authority the Scriptures exerted over the consciences of persons who believed they had found through their teachings the experience of salvation.

By the eve of the Civil War, the influence of biblical ideas in American culture was evident on every hand. As popular literature expanded beyond the explicitly religious forms of sermons, devotional manuals, and Sunday school lessons, American authors drew upon a common store of biblical narratives, poetry, ethical teachings, and apocalyptic visions—what Northrop Frye has called *the Great Code*. Popular writers embraced ancient Hebrew and Christian assumptions about human sin and its punishment in this life and the next and the promise and rewards of righteousness.

Numerous studies of school textbooks, travel guides, children's literature, newspaper editorials, and political oratory make this point clear, as do analyses of such things as self-help books, women's magazines, and Catholic novels. Intellectual historians have found biblical ideals pervasive also in the learned worlds of law, literature, science, and moral philosophy. Ralph Waldo Emerson, Louis Agassiz, and Herman Melville were as notably biblicists as Nathaniel Hawthorne, Frances Wayland, and Mark Hopkins. The rhetoric and the moral substance of court decisions and the speeches of such statesmen as John C. Calhoun, Daniel Webster, and Abraham Lincoln employed biblical teachings as vehicles of persuasion, certainly, if not always as sources of thought. Both defenders of the new industrialist class and champions of the workers whom they oppressed appealed to Moses and Jesus, as did the college men who lectured on political economy. And Americans who dreamed of the steady progress of their society toward the goals of justice and mutual love stated their ideology in millennial rhetoric drawn from the prophecy of Isaiah and the preaching of John the Baptist. The first generation of professional engineers, as Raymond Merritt has shown, built bridges, railway tunnels, water systems, and ocean docks in the conviction that commerce, science, education, democracy, and evangelical religion were engines of human progress set in motion by divine providence.

The "civil religion" of nineteenth-century America, displayed most profoundly in the later speeches of Abraham Lincoln, was cast in biblical terms. It found ready acceptance on all sides because it seemed in accord with the evangelical consensus about faith and ethics. True, Romanticism, flowing into the new nation from German and English sources but also generated in North American situations, drew deeply upon the spiritualizing tendencies of Platonic thought. But the Bible's Hebraic realism about social injustice and individual sin, about the human need for health, a good conscience, reward for toil, and the faithfulness of love, I think, was a far more powerful source of liberal political convictions.

In retrospect, this towering preeminence of the Bible over other past traditions, whether social, cultural, or religious, also opened the way for Jews and Roman Catholics to embrace the nation's ideals. Leaders of the German Jewish communities saw this earliest, I believe. During and just after the Civil War, Isaac Mayer Wise was able to draw together the majority of American rabbis in a movement called Reform Judaism. Wise's profound engagement with Scripture, his emphasis upon the Mosaic sources of law (rather outweighing, I think, his appreciation of the ethical idealism of the prophets), and his conviction that the mission of the Jews was to share both the ethics and the spirituality of Judaism with the non-Jewish world were the life and breath of Reform. He did not perceive his movement to represent either Americanization or secularization but rather a restoration of the essence of the law of Moses (to love God with all your heart and soul and strength, and to love your neighbor as yourself) and a recovery of the prophets' vision of a new

age of the spirit in which justice would pour down the mountain-
sides like a river.

When, toward the end of the century, Conservative rabbis reacted against the accelerating pace of accommodations to modern
culture, they also appealed to Scripture, and in a manner that Protestant evangelicals understood. In 1902, Cyrus Adler persuaded
young Solomon Schechter, a native of Romania and a lecturer in
Jewish studies at Cambridge University, to come to New York City
to head the Jewish Theological Seminary of America, and Conservative Jews found a leader. Schechter understood very well that the
immense investment of Protestant scholarship in studies of the Hebrew Bible during the previous hundred years opened the door to
full Jewish participation in America's biblical culture. At the dedication of the new seminary building in 1903, Schechter declared that
the United States was "a creation of the Bible, particularly of the Old
Testament." Jews could not only feel at home here, they could teach
the nation about God's covenant with them and his promise for all
humankind.

A parallel but less fully developed tendency appeared in Roman
Catholic circles. Here also such early leaders as Bishop John England
of Charleston, South Carolina, had affirmed American liberty, appealing to its biblical foundations. At mid-century, former
Methodist Isaac Hecker and one of Charles G. Finney's converts,
Clarence Walworth, were converted to Catholicism. They studied in
Rome and then returned to New York to found the Paulist Fathers,
devoted to preaching an intensely ethical and spiritual version of
Catholic faith to Protestant Americans. I think some recent students
of Hecker have overemphasized the Methodistic character of his
spirituality, particularly his preoccupation with sanctification. There
seems little doubt, however, that the "Americanist" party among the
Roman Catholic bishops recognized that a common scriptural foundation promised a growing rapprochement with Protestant America
despite the bitter history of anti-Catholic attitudes in the young nation.

Perhaps a small moral is now in order. Those who still believe
that America offers something valuable to the future of the world
should nurture here a pluralism that encourages each religious
group to affirm its own faith and declare it to all humankind. All of
us should rejoice in whatever good we can find in the others. And
all of us need all the help we can get in moving our race off its present suicidal course and redirecting it toward the righteousness and
shalom that is the work of the Spirit of God.

RELIGIOUS EXPERIENCE AND MORAL COMMITMENT

The experience of the new birth, which became an important theme in most denominations, endowed American idealism with the expectation of individual moral transformation. By the middle of the nineteenth century, the notion that young adults would pass through a period of heightened guilt over their moral inadequacies and find that guilt resolved in a crucial experience of faith or moral commitment was pervasive. Nonreligious sources of such an expectation are of course easy to identify, as witness Benjamin Franklin's *Autobiography*. But can we imagine that Franklin did not bring to his self-examination and commitment to self-discipline memories of the Puritan expectation of regenerating grace? Moralism in America has never been far removed from piety; and among the vast company of diverse evangelicals, it seemed organically connected to it, as fruit to a vine.

The ethical significance of the experience of the new birth in nineteenth-century Christianity needs to be reemphasized. In the twentieth century, popular preaching in many denominations minimized the notion of transforming grace and thus made room for a relaxation of moral discipline. Calvinistic evangelists from George Whitefield to Dwight Moody and pastors from Timothy Dwight to R. E. Torrey proclaimed that to be born again was to be freed not only from the guilt of sin but from bondage to its power, very much as Wesleyans did. The Holy Spirit who gave believers "new life in Christ" would lead them in the paths of righteousness. Young William Ellery Channing passed through just such an experience shortly after his graduation from Harvard in 1803. At an opposite pole, in Church of the Brethren circles young people were not expected to seek to be born again until their early twenties. At the end of a period of repentance and reflection that might last as much as six months, they found themselves able to trust in the redeeming power of Christ, confessed their faith, and committed themselves to the standards of behavior that this German Baptist denomination had practiced since the seventeenth century.

The experience of regeneration thus served as a moral rite of passage into the assumption of adult ethical responsibility. Nineteenth-century preachers, from Horace Bushnell to the priests who conducted preaching missions in Roman Catholic parishes, rarely failed to insist, as Moses and Jesus had, that loving God is inseparable from loving one's neighbor. The disengagement of these two summary commandments began only when the moral crusade against slavery produced among those who defended it a "spiritual" definition of salvation. Thereafter, Southern evangelicals—Presbyterians, Baptists, Lutherans, and, after a time, Methodists—gradually confined their moral concerns to abstinence from alcoholic beverages, gambling, illicit sex, theatergoing, and the like.

Seen thus in its actual nineteenth-century understanding, the experience of the new birth was a spiritual catalyst of major social movements, as I and many other historians have long argued. Gordon S. Wood, in his powerful reinterpretation of the movement for American independence, stressed the moral seriousness of the quest for virtue in republican ideology and rooted it not only in evangelical but in Enlightenment thought. My colleague John Pocock described and gently derided the emergence of the idea of public virtue with the phrase "a Machiavellian moment." I think, however, that the widespread devotion to the Hebrew Scriptures among colonial evangelicals of nearly all traditions, and their embrace of the idea of the new birth on the moral terms that John Wesley and George Whitefield laid out, suggests a better phrase: "the Mosaic moment." The alliance between evangelicals and Deists in the early stages of the revolutionary movement rested, as I see it, on a more solid foundation than some have believed—namely, the commitment of both parties to an ethic that was thoroughly biblical, even when defended on rational grounds. Thomas Jefferson's famous truncation of the ethical teachings of the New Testament in his "Bible" illustrates this fact.

In this light, I think, we can understand better the spiritual sources of the moral crusades of the nineteenth century, whether for common schools, against slavery, or for justice to the poor. Charles G. Finney and those who followed in his train insisted that their first ministry must be the conversion of sinners, for such conversion promised both the moral renewal of individuals and the presence and power of God to sustain Christians in a crusade for justice. Much later, Charles Howard Hopkins wrote in his *Rise of the Social Gospel* that despite the emergence in that movement of a corporate ideology, its fundamental method remained throughout the consecration of individuals and their resources to the will of God.

Such a view of conversion was accessible to both Roman Catholics and Jews, for it was rooted in the stories of decisive moral change that permeate the Hebrew as well as the Christian Scriptures. Jay Dolan's recent volume, *Catholic Revivalism*, shows that such an experience was what the Redemptorist priests aimed at in preaching missions in German Catholic parishes, using sermons and appeals developed for such missioners during preceding decades in Germany. Isaac Hecker's Paulist fathers sought the conversion of Protestants by stressing the intensely moral character of the life that was rooted in the sacraments and the spirituality of the Roman Catholic Church. Meanwhile, Reform rabbis who preached the spiritual and ethical mission of Judaism to Gentile culture often found the men of their congregations preoccupied with material success and the social advancement of their families. Especially in the solemn occasions of the Day of Atonement, but at other times as well, the rabbis called them back to the supreme dedication to the kingdom of God that the prophets had demanded. In Jewish understanding, that kingdom sought both justice in society and the moral perfection of individuals. At the end of the century, the leaders of the National Council of Jewish Women thought that teaching children, as one of them put it, "loving dependence upon the Creator, begotten of that sense of intimate relationship with him which constitutes the essence of spirituality" was the highest goal of religious education. The persistence of notions of dramatic moral transformation into our own times is apparent among such Jewish novelists as Bernard Malamud, whose novel *A New Life* records the frustration of one man's hope for a new beginning.

THE IDEOLOGY OF THE KINGDOM OF GOD ON EARTH

During the past thirty years, the discovery and widespread study of the significance of millennialism in nineteenth century America has yielded both affirmative and negative interpretations. But no one has questioned the close link of millennial ideology with mid-century evangelism or with the social vision that permeated Protestant Christianity in the decades after 1880. I have learned recently, with the help of two of my students, that millennial hopes also sparked the missionary and evangelistic movements that after 1795 spread from New York and Connecticut into the western frontier and throughout the nation. The notion of perfecting society, like the idea of the spiritual and moral perfection of individuals, was integral to these hopes, though more their result, I now believe, than their cause.

Two points remain unstressed, however. The first is the Hebraic character of the millennial vision, both during the early years of the nineteenth century and in the later social gospel movement. Only recently have scholars begun to grasp the broadly Hebraic character of the New Testament. The Hebrew sensibility, as contrasted with that of Hellenic Platonism, stressed the wholeness of human beings, the unity of their psychic and physical existence, and the bonds that link social experience to inward spirituality. The salvation promised in Torah, in the prophets, and in the Christian gospel reflects these outlooks: it offers to redeem both the bodies and the souls of individuals and the societies and cultures that nurture them. Biblical ethics, therefore, both Jewish and Christian, never divorce spirituality from acting justly (the literal meaning of the Hebrew word translated into English as "charity") on behalf of the poor or oppressed. The biblical idea of the millennium that such evangelicals as Samuel Hopkins and Methodist Gilbert Haven proclaimed, therefore, was, like much Jewish Messianism, social and political as well as spiritual.

Methodists in particular found this view sustained whenever they read John Wesley, which was most of the time. Wesley's salvation theology was grounded in the prophetic promise of the renewal of all creation that is to climax the age of the Spirit. In that day, all of created nature, like all human beings who in faith have embraced God's covenant of holiness, is to be made new in the perfection of the first creation, and heaven is to begin on earth. Edward Hopper's famous folk painting "The Peaceable Kingdom" caught the imagination of Americans precisely because it pictured so simply the least believable biblical symbol of that hope—lambs lying down with lions and sleeping very well at night. The conviction that millennial theology constituted realistic social ideology was not in the eyes of nineteenth-century evangelicals a distortion or diffusion of the biblical sources but a straightforward exposition of them. God's kingdom must prevail, cried Catherine Booth, cofounder with her husband of the Salvation Army, until divine grace has conquered not only all evil in human hearts but all injustice in human societies.

The other neglected point is the ecumenical character of millennial ideology: its proponents believed it to be a promise to the entire inhabited world. To be sure, from the time of the earliest settlement of America, Christians thought a special divine providence was at work in the opening of these new and unspoiled lands, and some of them saw a special mission for the United States in bringing forward the kingdom of God. Historians have made a great deal of a few scattered statements by Jonathan Edwards and others suggesting that America, the "new Canaan," was to be the center of the coming kingdom, and that the New Jerusalem would be located somewhere here. But a systematic reading of the literature of early nineteenth-century millennialism reveals that it constantly affirmed that the promises of the kingdom were for the entire human race. All parties insisted that God's redeeming purposes included not simply the "new Israel" of the Christian church but the Jews as a people. Even such a theological maverick as Joseph Smith, founder of the Church of Jesus Christ of the Latter-day Saints, taught that the New Jerusalem was to be built on the ruins of the Old.

This inclusive millennial vision inspired and sustained the foreign mission movement of the nineteenth century not only in the United States but in England, Scandinavia, and Germany as well. Its consequences are evident everywhere today—in Africa, Southeast Asia, and, as the Hebrew prophets had foreseen, "the islands of the sea." Demographers and futurists predict that sub-Saharan Africa will soon be the most Christianized of all the great populated regions of the world, and recent developments in South Korea and Indonesia sustain predictions of a similar outcome in much of the Orient as well.

Moreover, it is clear that the millennial ideal of theocracy permeated evangelism in this country as well as overseas. God would rule as the revelation of his steadfast love and the power of his sanctifying Spirit brought sinful persons into submission to his will. Christian missionaries, at home and abroad, did not think military or political power could be used to further the kingdom of God, but most of them believed that the growth of democracy in America and its spread to other nations would enable the future Christian majority to act in love and justice to produce a righteous society. Government of, by, and for the people, as Lincoln put it, was the hope of the earth. Evangelicals also believed that God was using other developments to move humanity toward the millennium: universal public education, advancements in science and technology, the liberation of women, and the prosperity stemming from international trade. Robert Frykenberg's account of how Christian missionaries to India in the eighteenth century resisted the conspiracy between the British East India Company and the Brahmin masters of that land to suppress the aspirations of the untouchables joins other recent studies to demonstrate the consistency between biblical, evangelical, and missionary ideology.

Millennial ideology was one source of interfaith pluralism. The notion of the transformation of society into a kingdom of justice and love was never far from the center of Jewish religious thought, whether in the universalist idealism of Reform, in the messianism that flowed out of medieval mysticism and spirituality, or in what Judah L. Magnes called spiritual Zionism. Magnes, who was from 1904 to 1909 associate rabbi of the nation's most eminent Reform congregation, Temple Emanu-El in New York City, discovered this fact during three previous years of study and spiritual reflection in Germany and Central Europe. He became at once both an uncompromising religious Zionist and the champion of what Christians might call a Hebrew social gospel. Rabbi Magnes spent the years after 1909 as head and guiding spirit of a communal movement that sought to unite all of New York City's Jews. He then moved by stages toward settling in the Holy Land, where he wound up as the longtime chancellor of the Hebrew University of Jerusalem. In 1907, Magnes was convinced that he stood biblically, morally, and spiritually on the same ground Isaac Mayer Wise had occupied fifty years before. Unlike Wise, however, he believed the mission of Jews to humankind must begin with a revitalization of their own faith and hope. He thought the Kehillah movement in New York and the establishment of a homeland in Palestine would help bring the Jews of the world, from Hasidic and Orthodox to the most radical party of Reform, to renew the covenant of righteous love. That covenant would bring holiness not only to their inner life but to all their relationships with non-Jewish peoples, including the Palestinian Arabs.

Ought we not to compare Magnes, whose eventual commitment to pacifism matched his love for Zion, with his great evangelical Protestant contemporary, John R. Mott? Mott became a leader in the Student Volunteer Movement and organized the World Christian Student Federation. He helped to shape the moral vision of God's rule on earth that revitalized the ecumenical movement and eventually brought Protestant and Eastern Orthodox Christians together in the World Council of Churches. Although popes John XXIII and John Paul II arrived late on this ecumenical scene—so late as to discover Protestant and Orthodox Christianity and Judaism as well in general retreat from the idea of a kingdom of God on earth—ought we not to regard them as in fact standing in the same tradition as Mott and Magnes and such beloved Eastern Orthodox ecumenists as Alexander Florovsky and Alexander Schmemann? If all this seems farfetched to you, I submit that one accomplishment of evangelical Protestants in nineteenth-century Canadian and American culture was to lay the foundations for what they hoped would become in the twentieth century a steady march toward peace and justice on earth. That hope called for shared commitment to biblical ethics and a shared confidence in the faithfulness of the Holy One of Israel. It made no place at all for the balancing of nuclear armaments or the manipulation of national economic interests that pass for peacemaking in our tragic times.

If this lecture, or sermon, or rabbinical discourse is to close, as all such declarations should, with an exhortation, mine is this: your first duty is to be truly what you are, to drink again from the wells dug by your father Abraham, to let the Holy Scriptures speak their persisting message of *shalom* to your own mind and heart. If you will, the evangelical Christians, Eastern or Roman Catholics, and Jews you represent or can influence may learn how to stand together on biblical principles of righteousness. And if that happens, the leaders of not only North America and Israel but of the nations we fear may find a way out of our present social, moral, and political darkness into the dawning light of a new age.

American Protestantism: Sorting out the Present, Looking toward the Future

James Davison Hunter

To speak of the future of American religion is to speak of the future of particular moral visions. These are, of course, institutionalized within ecclesiastical and extraecclesiastical structures, supported variously by a constituency and promulgated by an elite. At the heart, however, they are moral visions and their future remains elusive.

In the past the fate of moral visions was never determined solely or even mainly by their inherent truth or by the power of their internal logic but rather by their affinities with pragmatic interests and concerns institutionalized within different sectors of the social order and by the degree of stability and change of particular social structures. The same can be said for the fate of these moral visions within our own generation. The quest for truth and the sophistication of apologetic, in the final analysis, may have little to do with their ultimate success or failure—their longevity or their demise. All of this is to say that the future of religion is and has been, in large part, a political question—linked in important ways to demographic, structural, and even cultural factors to be sure, but a political question all the same. The future of religion, then, is linked to its future in the public square and linked to the future of the public square itself.

The political factor has always been central in determining the fate of any moral vision, but the nature of the political factor has altered over the last several decades. It is not as though the social context in which the fate of religion is decided has become more politicized but rather that it is becoming more openly or more explicitly politicized. I believe that this is due to a restructuring of the major cultural axes of American life. In short, the nature and structure of moral pluralism has shifted. And what is the significance of pluralism? Whatever else it has come to mean, pluralism now entails a competition on the part of different moral traditions to define reality. The nature of that competition, I would suggest, has altered in recent times, and this has had and will continue to have important consequences for the fate of religion.

The question, then, concerns the nature of contemporary moral pluralism and the competition it implies as well as the major factors determining the outcome of this competition. While it would be possible to explore cultural conflict generally in America, my main interest will be with the ways in which this larger conflict is reflected in the mosaic of American religion and, in particular, the mosaic of American Protestantism. Such an approach may provide an interpretive means through which credible speculation about the future of American Protestantism can take place.

PLURALISM IN AMERICAN RELIGIOUS LIFE

Historical and Contemporary Divisions

At least through the heart of the nineteenth century, biblical theism strongly influenced if not defined the legitimating myth of American society. It permeated republican political rhetoric;[1] dominated the ideology of common school and later public school[2] and higher education;[3] imprinted the ethos of community, work, and family life;[4] spawned vast structures of social welfare;[5] and provided the

---

1. See Nathan O. Hatch, *The Sacred Cause of Liberty: Republican Thought and the Millennium in Revolutionary New England* (New Haven: Yale University Press, 1977); and James West Davidson, *The Logic of Millennial Thought: Eighteenth-Century New England* (New Haven: Yale University Press, 1977).

2. See Timothy Smith, "Protestant Schooling and American Nationality, 1800-1850," *The Journal of American History* 53 (March 1967): 679-95.

3. See Mark Noll, "Christian Thinking and the Rise of the American University," *Christian Scholars Review* 9 (1979): 3-16; and Richard Hofstadter, "The Revolution in Higher Education," in *Paths of American Thought*, ed. Arthur M. Schlesinger Jr. and Morton White (Boston: Houghton Mifflin, 1970).

4. See Phillip Greven, *The Protestant Temperament* (New York: Knopf, 1977); Donald Mathews, *Religion in the Old South* (Chicago: University of Chicago Press, 1977); and Daniel Bell, *The Cultural Contradictions of Capitalism* (New York: Basic Books, 1976).

5. See Timothy Smith, "Biblical Ideals in American Christian and Jewish Philanthropy, 1880-1920," *American Jewish History* 74 (September 1984): 3-26.

primary institutions and ideals through which an expanding and increasingly diverse immigrant population (Protestant, Catholic, and Jewish) adapted to a new life in America.[6] It is of course true that biblical theism was based on sectarian commitment and was overwhelmingly Protestant in character, but the larger cultural order was sufficiently diffuse to allow for the participation of other biblical traditions. At least through this period, religious and cultural pluralism were defined *within* the boundaries of this deeply biblical culture.

Needless to say, the common moral heritage provided by biblical theism did not mean all was placid in American cultural life. First and most obviously, sharp sectarian division existed *among* broad religious traditions. Indigenous anti-Catholic sentiment, for example, was widespread in the nineteenth century, originally in the nativist, anti-Masonic, and Know-Nothing movements; it was evident in the postbellum period particularly in such organizations as the National Christian Association (1868), the American Alliance (1876) and the American Protective Association (1887), as the wave of East European and Irish (mainly Catholic) immigrants arriving on American shores grew. It is true that much of the anti-Catholic hostility was born out of economic frustration and ethnic distrust, but it largely took expression as religious hostility—as a quarrel over religious doctrine, practice, and authority. Anti-Romanist rhetoric repeatedly denounced the pope and the Roman Catholic Church for conspiring to subvert American institutions. Catholics were not quiescent in the face of all this, as the Catholic school movement suggests. Importantly, the Catholic hierarchy's push for public funds for parochial schools was based not on an objection to the overt theism that distinguished the educational ideology of public schools but rather to the bold sectarian (i.e., Protestant) character of that theism.[7] Anti-Jewish sentiment was also present, but because the first major wave of Jewish immigrants to this country did not come until the 1880s, it was far less pronounced than anti-Catholicism. It did brew quietly in the nineteenth century, however, as seen

---

6. See Timothy Smith, "Immigrant Social Aspirations and American Education, 1800-1930," *The American Quarterly* 21 (Fall 1969): 523-43; and "Religion and Ethnicity in America," *The American Historical Review* 83 (December 1978): 1155-85. See also *Immigrants and Religion in Urban America*, ed. Randall M. Miller and Thomas D. Marzik (Philadelphia: Temple University Press, 1977).

7. Cross, 1968; Dohen, 1967.

in agrarian populist resentment against the "Hebrew conquest" of the financial centers of the East,[8] and this latent bigotry, too, was religiously legitimated. Clearly the Protestant hostility toward Jews was not in fact based on an opposition to their belief in a beneficent Deity or their (religiously based) optimism for the American future, for these things Protestants and Jews largely had in common; rather, as with the Catholics, the Protestant objection was most often rooted in ethnic distrust but expressed in the language of religious antipathy.

In the nineteenth century, sectarian division *within* religious traditions defined another significant aspect of religio-cultural pluralism. Within American Protestantism, for example, denominational schism has been one of its defining characteristics from the beginning—and, indeed, one reason it has prospered so. On the other hand, denominational rivalries very often also served to nurture deep resentments that were sometimes expressed in policies of exclusion. The pride of denominational heritage produced divisions. Doctrinal issues that cut across denominational lines (e.g., pietism, dispensationalism, and the "infidelity" of universalism) produced divisions. Social issues (most prominently slavery and abolition) produced divisions. All of these issues, including the social issues of the day, were typically defined in religious if not theological language. The Jewish experience provides another example of this kind of internal factionalizing. Two factors—the transplantation of the Reform movement from Europe (in the 1840s) and its subsequent growth, and the formation and expansion of the Conservative movement in the mid-1880s—had by the the end of the nineteenth century reduced Orthodox Jews to a beleaguered minority. Here again, though, pluralism within Judaism was manifested in different styles of ritual observance and in the degree of universality of its ethical vision.

It goes without saying that the divisions within and among the Protestant, Catholic, and Jewish traditions were very often rooted in ethnicity, geography, and social class. Nevertheless, to the communities involved these divisions were almost invariably understood in religious terms; that is to say, the divisions were typically articulated within a common moral language—a form of discourse

---

8. See John Higham, "Social Discrimination against Jews in America, 1830-1930," *American Jewish Historical Society* 47 (1957): 1-33; and "Anti-Semitism in the Gilded Age: A Reinterpretation," *Mississippi Valley Historical Review* 43 (1957): 559-78.

shaped in large part by the symbols of biblical theism. Another way of putting this is to say that pluralism in American life, at least through the heart of the nineteenth century, revolved mainly around the cultural axes of doctrine and ecclesia. Importantly, these divisions (among Protestant, Catholic, and Jew and to a lesser extent formal ecclesiastical divisions within these faiths) were the significant ones not only in the popular imagination but in early European and American social science as well. In both the popular mind and in academia these divisions have provided the primary mechanism for thinking about religious/cultural diversity and for measuring its comparative significance.

With a few exceptions, mainly in the sociology of religion proper, social science has continued over the past two decades to treat religious/cultural pluralism in this way, holding on to these categories as the key to thinking about religious pluralism. Using this methodology, social science has also gradually come to document religion's declining significance as an explanatory variable. They give little evidence of taking traditional divisions (between, say, Protestants, Catholics, and Jews) into account in their attitudinal research, and as a result the larger social scientific community has come to assume that religion really is epiphenomenal. In much of the most recent research, religious variables are not even included in analysis.

The social science establishment, in my view, is mistaken. The principal reason religion no longer appears to be salient in many empirically oriented studies is that the older divisions have become less and less important. Religious pluralism has taken on new and tremendously meaningful forms that the social scientific establishment has failed to take into account either theoretically or methodologically. The primary axis defining religious and cultural pluralism in American life has shifted. The important divisions are no longer ecclesiastical but rather "cosmological." They no longer revolve around specific doctrinal issues or styles of religious practice and organization but rather around fundamental assumptions about values, purpose, truth, freedom, and collective identity. More to the point, contemporary pluralism is centered in the sources of moral authority in the social order. The collapse of a common ascription to biblical theism, as diffuse as that ascription was, meant the loss of a common moral authority. What remains is an intensifying struggle to generate a source of moral authority acceptable to all, and with it the common terms of public discourse and the dominant symbols of national life.

A few clarifying observations are in order. First, in the context of

American religion (and in many respects, the larger culture) the poles of this cultural axis are orthodoxy and progressivism. Yet orthodoxy and progressivism are not substantive categories (associated with specific doctrine) but rather formal properties. In substantive terms, for example, orthodoxy is defined in vastly different ways within different religious traditions. Within Judaism it is defined mainly by commitment to Torah and the community that upholds it; within Catholicism it is defined largely by loyalty to church teaching; and within Protestantism it is defined principally by devotion to the spiritual prerogatives of Scripture. What is common to all three approaches to orthodoxy, however, and what makes orthodoxy more of a formal property, is the commitment on the part of votaries to an external, definable, and transcendent authority. Such authority defines, at least in the abstract, a consistent unchangeable measure of value, purpose, goodness, and identity, both personal and collective. It is an authority that is sufficient for all time.

At the opposite pole of this cultural axis is progressivism. The term is somewhat imprecise, but it is suggestive.[9] Here again, the term should not be understood substantively, for on these grounds there is wide variability. What the term suggests is that moral authority is defined by the spirit of the age. Progressivist moral visions derive from and embody (though rarely exhaust) that spirit. Insofar as the larger religious community is concerned, traditional moral visions are made to conform to and legitimate the *Zeitgeist*. In other words, what all progressivist programs have in common is the resymbolization of historic faiths. Underlying most contemporary progressivist cosmologies are assumptions that tend toward naturalism and/or subjectivism.

Within Protestantism, of course, the poles of this axis are formalized in the division between the fundamentalist/evangelical churches on the one hand and the mainline/liberal churches on the other. Within Judaism they are formalized in the division between Orthodoxy/Modern Orthodoxy on the one hand and the Reform

---

9. One reason the term is not totally satisfactory is that many associate it with a political movement and ideology. It also connotes a positive development that many would find debatable. Yet the search for alternate terms leads to other problems. The antonyms of *orthodoxy*—*heterodoxy* or *heresy*—connote too much. A word such as *revisionism* is problematic for similar reasons, implying as it does a departure from truth. The issue is not the distinction between truth and falsehood but between different interpretations of truth—interpretations that differ because the criteria (or authority) established to measure correct interpretation differ.

movement on the other (with Conservativism somewhere in be-tween). The poles have not been formalized within Catholicism ex-cept in the development of different and opposing religio-political coalitions in the larger Catholic community.[10]

We might also take note of the rather strong affinity between moral reasoning and political ideology. In particular, I am referring to the relationship between moral and religious preservationism and political conservativism on the one hand, and moral and religious liberalism and political progressivism on the other. It would be fool-ish, of course, to elevate these relationships to the status of a social axiom holding for all times and for all places. There are of course politically liberal evangelical elites and politically conservative mainline elites—but they tend to be the exception rather than the rule. Overall, the affinities are too reliable to only be coincidental.

A third observation is more conjecture than established fact: within American religion and within the broader culture, there seems to be a tendency toward polarization along the cultural axis I have been describing. Very simply, the poles of this cultural axis are becoming increasingly crystallized in opposition to each other. The process is anything but complete, but it is taking place, and it is serv-ing to make the politicized nature of the Protestant future more open and explicit.

Even if I am only partially correct in these observations, then it seems clear that we cannot project the future of American Protes-tantism in terms of its own internal dynamics alone—that is, in isolation from larger social and cultural developments. The future of American Protestantism will be played out in the context of a larger cultural conflict. The precise nature of this conflict (particularly as it is reflected in Protestantism) becomes more evident if we consider ecumenism in the post–World War II period. An analysis of ecu-menism provides compelling evidence for the hypothesis of a cul-tural realignment.

The Changing Meaning of Ecumenism

If, in sociological terms, moral pluralism implies a competition to

---

10. On the orthodox side one could mention the Catholic Tradition-alist Movement (1964), Catholics United for the Faith (1968), Charismatic Renewal Services (1971), and the Catholic League for Civil and Religious Rights (1973). On the progressivist side one could mention the higher echelons of the Catholic leadership (including the American Catholic bishops) as well as Dignity, Catholics for ERA, and so on.

define reality, then ecumenism can be understood as a form of cooperative mobilization. Previously distinct and separate religious and moral traditions share resources and work together toward common objectives. Pluralism and ecumenism, then, are very nearly opposite structural tendencies. They need to be understood relative to each other. For this reason I would suggest that if the structure of religious pluralism is changing, the nature of religious cooperation must be changing as well. But in what ways?

The conventional academy wisdom about ecumenism is that it has been a strategy adopted by the mainline religious bodies to defend against a hostile secular environment.[11] It is supposed to reduce the number of "competing units," allowing those that remain to compete more effectively for adherents. The logic is difficult to quarrel with. And perhaps the ecumenical movement did indeed begin with such aims in view, but I would contend that it has since evolved into a much more encompassing social process. Consider, for example, that within Protestantism, both the mainline and evangelical/fundamentalist wings have engaged in aggressive forms of ecumenical activity. The function of this ecumenical activity, I would argue, has not only been to mobilize against the onslaught of secular modernity but to marshal resources against each other and, more importantly, against the larger cultural forces the other side represents. This assertion requires some elaboration.

Two more or less distinct strategies of ecumenical cooperation among Protestants have been pursued in the post–World War II period—a church-unity strategy and a project-oriented strategy. The terms are not terribly elegant or precise but they are descriptive and perhaps useful for the present purposes. The church-unity strategy has chiefly involved the effort to achieve organizational unity (e.g., the formation of new denominations from two or more older denominations); cooperation among ecclesiastical organizations through umbrella organizations would also fall into this category. The project-oriented strategy has aimed at the transcendence of ecclesiastical divisions altogether through a common commitment to particular religious projects and goals (e.g., world evangelism, campus ministry, publishing, education, and the like).

---

11. See Peter L. Berger, "A Market Model for the Analysis of Ecumenicity," *Sociology and Social Research* 30 (Spring 1963): 77-93; Samuel Cavert, *The American Churches and the Ecumenical Movement, 1900-1968* (New York: Associated Press, 1968); and Talcott Parsons, "Religion in Postindustrial America: The Problem of Secularization," *Social Research* 41 (1974): 193-225.

With few exceptions, the orthodox wing of Protestantism has shown little interest in the church-unity strategy. Only 8 percent of all new conservative denominations (eleven denominations in all) have formed from merger since 1945 (see Table 1). The largest of these mergers have been those that brought about the expansion of the Evangelical Free Church in 1950 (70,000 members),[12] the Lutheran Church–Missouri Synod in 1963 (2.5 million members),[13] and the Reformed Presbyterian Church, Evangelical Synod in 1965 (25,000 members).[14] All other mergers were among very small pietistic and holiness denominations. Beyond this there have arisen a number of umbrella organizations such as the National Association of Evangelicals, the American Council of Christian Churches, the Independent Fundamentalist Churches of America, the Independent Fundamentalist Bible Churches, and the National Association of Holiness Churches. With the exception of the NAE and the ACCC, these organizations have, for all practical purposes, been apolitical and hence publicly invisible.

In general, then, the tendency within the conservative family of denominations has been quite the opposite of bureaucratic unity. Organizationally, the orthodox wing of Protestantism has become even more factionalized: more than 120 new (even if typically quite small) conservative denominations have been formed since 1945. A split within the Southern Baptist Convention would add still another to this list.

At this point, an observation: if ecumenism were expressed only in bureaucratic cooperation and unification, then the orthodox wing of Protestantism could be seen as disorganized, incohesive, and splintered. Yet even those with only a superficial knowledge of the movement know that just the opposite is true. The reason is that the most significant ecumenical activity has been extraecclesiastical; it has taken shape in the development of a massive structure of independent parachurch organizations.[15] These organizations have become so expansive that virtually every area of social life has an evangelical parallel: primary and secondary schools, colleges, uni-

---

12. From the Swedish Evangelical Free Church and the Norwegian-Danish Evangelical Free Church Association.

13. This expansion occurred with the inclusion of the National Evangelical Lutheran Church in 1963.

14. From the merger of the Evangelical Presbyterian Church and the Reformed Presbyterian Church, General Synod.

15. See Richard G. Hutcheson, Jr., *Mainline Churches and the Evangelicals: A Challenging Crisis?* (Atlanta: John Knox Press, 1981).

Table 1
ECUMENICAL AND SECTARIAN ACTIVITY AND THE GENERATION OF NEW DENOMINATIONS IN EVANGELICAL AND MAINLINE PROTESTANTISM BETWEEN 1945 AND 1985

| | Protestant Tradition | |
	Evangelical Protestant (N = 142)	Mainline Protestant (N = 10)
Source of New Denomination		
Denominations formed from merger	8%	60%
Denominations formed from schism	59	30
Brand new denomination	33	10

SOURCES: J. Gordon Melton, *The Encyclopedia of American Religions* (Wilmington, N.C.: McGrath, 1978); *The Encyclopedia of American Religions—Supplement* (Detroit: Gale Research, 1985); and *A Directory of Religious Bodies in the United States* (New York: Garland, 1977).

METHODOLOGICAL NOTE: When new denominations were formed over doctrinal or polity differences, classification (into mainline or evangelical) derived from the "direction" of the split. That is, if the new denomination was formed over a substantial rejection of theological liberalization and political radicalization in the larger denomination, it was placed in the evangelical category. If the new denomination was formed over a fundamental rejection of conservative doctrine or polity, it was placed in the mainline camp. In many cases the divisions resulted from minor doctrinal disputes or personality clashes, but the new denomination remained fundamentally conservative or fundamentally liberal. (This was particularly true of the new denominations in the Holiness and Pentecostal families.)

versities, think tanks, publishing houses, periodicals, bookstores, social work agencies, law firms, businesses, international relief agencies, dating services, music companies, and professional organizations (supporting everyone from physicians to cowboys), not to mention a myriad of evangelistic organizations. Indeed, parachurch organizations have become such a prominent part of the conservative Protestant world that the words *parachurch* and *evangelical* have virtually become synonymous.[16]

Most significantly for the case I am making here, this kind of extraecclesiastical ecumenism has even extended *beyond* the religious boundaries of evangelical Protestantism to incorporate other religious and cultural orthodoxies. This has been particularly true as evangelicalism has confronted the public square and sought to preserve if not extend its interests through issues of broader moral con-

---

16. I thank Joel Carpenter for this observation.

cern. Opposition to legalized abortion in the Right-to-Life movement was perhaps the first issue upon which religiously orthodox Protestants, Catholics, and Jews formed alliances, but since 1973 a much larger, broader, and more complex network of conservative moral organizations has evolved. It is even possible to speak of a loose coalition among morality-in-media organizations (e.g., groups fighting pornography, rock music, and objectionable television programming), profamily organizations (e.g., Right-to-Life, anti-ERA, parents' rights groups), and nationalistic organizations (e.g., constitutional groups, anticommunist groups). Many of these groups are evangelical, many are Catholic, a few are Jewish, and many are nonsectarian. Yet they communicate with each other and even draw direct support from each other. For example, in an informal survey of forty-seven of these public affairs organizations,[17] I found that all claimed to be in communication with individuals or groups outside of their own religious or philosophical tradition, and most reported that they had engaged in active cooperation. The overwhelming majority of these organizations were supported by grass-roots contributions, and of these all but one or two claimed to receive con-

---

17. I conducted this survey during the first two weeks of October 1986. The organizations included were the Catholic League for Religious and Civil Rights; Liberty Federation; the Roundtable; Morality in Media; Eagle Forum; Prison Fellowship; the National Right-to-Life Committee; the American Catholic Conference; the American Catholic Committee; the American Coalition for Traditional Values; Christian Voice; the American Society for the Defense of Tradition, Family, and Property; Coalitions for America; Christian Citizen's Crusade; Conservative Caucus; the Foundation for Religious Action in the Social and Civil Order; the Jewish Right; the National Pro-Family Coalition; the National Traditionalist Caucus; the Order of the Cross Society; Parents Alliance to Protect Our Children; the Ethics and Public Policy Center; the Institute on Religion and Democracy; Religious Heritage of America; Rock Is Stoning Kids; Students for America; United Parents under God; American Life Lobby; Christian Action Council; Human Life International; Association for Public Justice; Voice of Liberty Association; Methodists for Life; Catholics United for Life; Human Life Center; Pro-Family Forum; Center on Religion and Society; American Pro-Life Council; the National Federation for Decency; Americans for Life; Concerned Women for America; Fund for an American Renaissance; We the People; the Ad Hoc Committee for the Defense of Life; the National League of Catholic Laymen; the American Council for Coordinated Action; and the Black Silent Majority. In all but a few cases, I had a telephone interview with a representative of these organizations. In some instances, though, enough information was provided in the description of the organization in the *Encyclopedia of Associations*.

tributions from Protestants, Catholics, the Eastern Orthodox, and Jews. Finally, roughly half of these groups sought to make explicit and public their commitment to coalition formation (i.e., to the larger ecumenism) by deliberately including representation from the range of traditions on their organization's board of advisors or board of trustees.

One of the significant features of this ecumenism is that alliances are being generated among traditions that have historically been antagonistic toward one another. The traditional divisions have been superseded as alliances that have been historically "unnatural" have become pragmatically necessary. Even so, a measure of tension and suspicion remains (particularly between conservative Catholic groups working with evangelical and fundamentalist groups). The tension appears to be tolerated, though, and justified by the dictum that "an enemy of an enemy is a friend of mine."

In the mainline Protestant denominations ecumenism takes shape in a somewhat different way. The mainline churches do engage in project-oriented ecumenism within a structure of parachurch organizations of course, but not nearly so frequently or enthusiastically as is the case in the evangelical wing. They tend to follow the church-unity model of ecumenism a good deal more. This is perhaps best illustrated by the formation of new denominations in the mainline: 60 percent of the new denominations in the progressive wing of Protestantism have come from bureaucratic mergers. The actual number of mergers may be small (only six since 1945), but the number of people represented in these mergers is quite large: the Lutheran Church in America merger (1962) involved 3 million members; the American Lutheran Church merger (1961) involved 2.2 million members; the United Church of Christ merger (1961) involved 2.2 million members; the United Methodist Church merger (1968) involved 10.5 million members; the United Presbyterian Church of the United States merger (1958) involved 3.1 million members; and the Presbyterian Church (USA) merger (1983) involved 3.1 million members.

Concomitant with this has been the expansion of the bureaucratic umbrella of the National Council of Churches since World War II. Contrary to its orthodox counterparts, the NCC has consolidated enormous political and financial resources and, as such, has become a formidable political presence.

The more interesting and significant ecumenical activity in the mainline traditions, though, has been outside of these formal denominational structures—in the coalitions that transcend historical antagonisms, among mainline Protestants, liberal Catholics, Jews, and secularists. As with their orthodox counterparts, these mainline groups join to assert their pragmatic interests as a larger moral community responding to specific issues. Their alliances take shape most visibly in the ecclesiastical involvement and major financial commitment of the National Council of Churches and several mainline denominations (independently) to such left-of-center, multifaith organizations as the North American Congress on Latin America, the Washington Office on Latin America, the Committee in Solidarity with the People of El Salvador, the Ecumenical Program for Inter-American Communication and Action, the Center for Constitutional Rights, Clergy and Laity Concerned, Coalition for a New Foreign and Military Policy, the Religious Task Force on Central America, the Inter-Religious Task Force on El Salvador and Central America, Theology in the Americas, the Indochina Consortium of the World Council of Churches, CAREE (Christians Associated for Relationships with Eastern Europe), the Fellowship of Reconciliation, and the Interfaith Center for Corporate Responsibility.[18]

Both the orthodox and progressivist wings of Protestantism have followed intense if unwitting strategies of ecumenical cooperation in the period since World War II. Their alliances extend within and beyond their respective theological traditions and reflect the practical necessities of an increasingly crystallized cultural realignment.[19] Interestingly, this realignment is reflected not only institutionally but attitudinally as well. As one recent study of Protestant and Catholic theologians concluded, "Mainline Protestant theologians share more in common [in terms of a general political and moral *Weltanschauung*] with those on the opposite side of the Reformation (Catholic theologians) than they do with those on the same side of the Reformation (Evangelical theologians)."[20] Other studies support

---

18. The complexities of these alliances have been documented in some detail in Appendix One of *The Betrayal of the Church*, by Edmund W. Robb and Julia Robb (Westchester, Ill.: Crossway, 1986). The financial underwriting of these organizations by the National Council of Churches, the World Council of Churches, and many of the major mainline denominations varies considerably, from thousand-dollar grants to grants totalling in the hundreds of thousands—millions over the course of two to three years.

19. I am of course describing the evolving structure of religious and cultural pluralism analytically. The poles are ideal types that reflect more opposing impulses or tendencies than empirical realities. Continua (shaped in part by such factors as social class, region, etc.) define either end of the axis.

20. See J. D. Hunter, James Tucker, and Steven Finkel, "Religious

the larger principle that the historical divisions have been super-seded.

A CLASH OF CULTURES:
THE STRUGGLE TO DEFINE THE FUTURE

The need for commonly held ideals to sustain a national identity, the practical necessity for a universal system of law and justice, and the desirability of a common heritage within which to educate succeeding generations of children all create a certain demand for moral clarity in the larger social order. For these reasons alone, social systems continually strive to find and maintain commonly held symbols—symbols that make collective life possible. As I have already noted, the current cultural conflict—what Richard Neuhaus and Peter Berger have called a *Kulturkampf*[21]—centers on what those symbols will be and the manner in which they will be interpreted. It amounts to a struggle to define the future.

If this is so, it means that American culture is in something of a transition. The question is what will determine the outcome. As I have suggested, it is naive to assume that the truthful position will prevail, that things will simply work out for the best for all concerned. Under these circumstances it is equally naive to imagine that a rational negotiated settlement will take place. In fact, this is more than just theoretically implausible; it is more nearly a sociological impossibility. For one thing, the most zealous advocates at either end of the cultural axis are not inclined to work for a genuinely pluralistic resolution; if anything, they are inclined to do precisely the opposite. The rhetoric employed by both extremes exaggerates the power and intentions of the opposition. It also uses the language of American ideals in an attempt to monopolize the symbols of legitimacy and discredit the positions if not the very existence of the opposition. Indeed, if one takes the rhetoric at all seriously, both sides operate upon policies of exclusion; both sides are intolerant of a pluralism that would incorporate the other. Both sides, then, betray the markings of moral bigotry in their rejection of the legitimacy of op-

---

Elites and Political Values," unpublished manuscript, University of Virginia, 1986.

21. See Neuhaus, *The Naked Public Square* (Grand Rapids: Eerdmans, 1984); and Berger, "American Religion: Conservative Upsurge, Liberal Prospects," in *Liberal Protestantism*, ed. Robert Michaelsen and Wade Clark Roof (New York: Pilgrim, 1986).

posing moral perspectives. The net effect of all of this, of course, is the creation of a political climate of deep suspicion and fear.[22]

The question of whether there will be an eventual resolution of this "war of dogmas" will depend on the kinds of power and resources each end of the cultural axis can assemble on behalf of its cause. Needless to say, not every moral vision has the same power and the same resources. Within Protestantism a number of factors will weigh significantly in determining the final outcome. For the present I will tentatively pursue four of these.

The Laity: The Demographic Factor

One widely held assumption about social movements is that the number of adherents is directly related to the amount of power the movement wields. Whether or not this is true, it does not tell us very much. In Protestantism, for example, general estimates put the number in the mainline at roughly 83 million, or 35 percent of the American population. For evangelicals/fundamentalists it is approximately 52 million, or 22 percent of the general population. If these figures are correct, the power of the former should far overshadow that of the latter. But the fact is that the figures do not provide us with a real picture of the general trends.

From the first publication of Dean Kelley's astute book *Why Conservative Churches Are Growing* in 1972 (it was reissued in 1977), there has been a virtual consensus among scholars that since some point in the mid-1960s, the mainline denominations have been declining and the conservative denominations have been in ascendance.[23] In absolute numbers the general tendencies have not changed (see Table 2). First consider the mainline. Since 1965 the United Methodist Church has lost 1.6 million members; the Presbyterian Church (USA) has lost just under a million members; the Episcopal Church has lost 65,000 members and the United Church of Christ has lost a quarter million members. By contrast in the same period

---

22. I develop this argument more fully in "The Liberal Reaction," in *The New Christian Right: Mobilization and Legitimation*, ed. Robert Liebman and Robert Wuthnow (New York: Aldine, 1983).

23. See, for example, *Understanding Church Growth and Decline, 1950-1978*, ed. Dean Hoge and David Roozen (New York: Pilgrim, 1979); Gallup Opinion Index, *Religion in America* (Princeton: Princeton Religious Research Center, 1977); and Wade Clark Roof, "America's Voluntary Establishment: Mainline Religion in Transition," *Daedelus*, Winter 1982, pp. 165-84.

Table 2
CHURCH MEMBERSHIP TRENDS IN SELECTED MAINLINE AND EVANGELICAL DENOMINATIONS

	1965	1975	1984
Mainline			
United Methodist Church	11,067,497	9,861,028	9,405,164*
United Church of Christ	2,070,413	1,818,762	1,696,107
Presbyterian Church (U.S.A.)	3,984,460	3,535,825	3,092,151
Episcopal Church	3,429,153	2,857,513	2,775,424
Evangelical			
Southern Baptist Convention	10,770,573	12,733,124	14,341,822
Assemblies of God	572,123	785,348	1,189,143
Salvation Army	287,991	384,817	420,971
Church of God (Cleveland, Tenn.)	205,465	343,249	505,775
Christian & Missionary Alliance	64,586	145,833	223,141

Source: *Yearbook of American and Canadian Churches, 1986,* ed. Constant H. Jacquet, Jr. (Nashville: Abingdon Press, 1986).

the Southern Baptist Convention membership increased by 3.6 million, the Salvation Army increased by 130,000 (significant, given its size in 1965), the Church of God (Cleveland, Tenn.) and the Assemblies of God have both more than doubled their numerical size, and the Christian and Missionary Alliance has more than tripled its membership. These figures point to a tendency that holds true for a much larger cast of denominations.

These demographic trends provide one of the main reasons for the orgy of self-congratulation that conservative Protestants have been indulging in since the mid-1970s. But there is another way of considering the demographic factor that may not contradict the earlier projections but does substantially qualify them. This other story is told by trends in the *growth rate* of the two major factions in Protestantism. This is summarized in Figure 1 (on p. 34).

Once again, it is not as though Kelley and others who posit conservative growth and liberal decline are incorrect. As the figures show, a substantial part of the church growth can be explained by the growth in the American population as a whole. When this demographic variable is held constant (or factored out), conservative church growth is not nearly so dramatic. But whether or not one does this, one can observe a trend in the "growth rate": overall the average growth rate of conservative Protestant denominations has

Figure 1
MEMBERSHIP GROWTH AND DECLINE IN EVANGELICAL AND MAINLINE DENOMINATIONS, 1940-1983
(Five-Year Moving Averages)

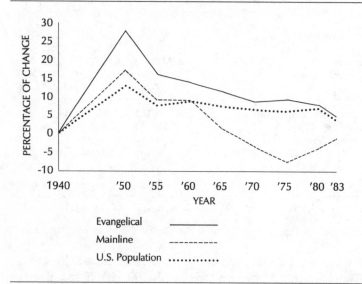

Evangelical —————

Mainline ----------

U.S. Population ············

Source: J. D. Hunter, *Evangelicalism: The Coming Generation* (Chicago: University of Chicago Press, 1987), p. 205.

shown a fairly steady decline since the 1940s.[24] There was a slight increase in the growth rate between 1970 and 1975, but this trend reversed in the years following.[25]

What does all of this mean? It first means that the religious revival some assume to have taken place in the 1970s, bringing in large numbers of new believers, was in fact very slight if it took place at all. It is true, as Figure 1 shows, that the church membership growth

24. These data are derived from the 1985 edition of the *Yearbook of American and Canadian Churches*. For a listing of the denominations included in Figure 1 and the actual numbers used to determine growth rate, see J. D. Hunter, *Evangelicalism: The Coming Generation* (Chicago: University of Chicago Press, 1987), chap. 8, n. 2.

25. William R. Hutchison recently made a similar argument in his essay "Past Imperfect: History and the Prospect for Liberalism," in *Liberal Protestantism: Realities and Possibilities*, ed. Robert S. Michaelsen and Wade Clark Roof (New York: Pilgrim Press, 1986), pp. 65-82.

rate did increase marginally between 1970 and 1975. It is also true that this increase took place at the same time that membership in mainline churches was undergoing a fairly precipitous decline. But this in itself hardly constitutes a national revival. Besides, what real church growth did take place may have had less to do with bringing in *new* believers than it did with a certain "circulation" of "old" believers, either through the retention of geographically mobile members and offspring or else through the process of denominational "switching"—changing one's denominational affiliation though staying in the conservative Protestant orbit. In other words, while there had been some church growth in the 1970s and 1980s, the growth may have been more internal (due to geographic mobility, higher birthrate, and recent immigration)[26] than external (due to proselytization). The real revival of the 1970s, then, may have been more of a cultural phenomenon than a numerical phenomenon—a revival of public awareness about evangelicalism due in part to the extraordinary attention it received from the mass media.

In the end these figures merely temper the popular excitement or worry (depending on one's perspective) about conservative growth and liberal decline. Decline in the moderate and liberal denominations appears to have leveled off considerably, and conservative growth is not nearly as dramatic as it once was. In the long run, the evangelical/fundamentalist contingent may gain a certain numerical parity with the mainline, but at best this would be a long time away.

---

26. On geographic mobility, see two articles by Reginald Bibby and Merlin Brinkerhoff, "The Circulation of the Saints," *Journal for the Scientific Study of Religion* 12 (1973): 273-85; and "The Circulation of the Saints Revisited," *Journal for the Scientific Study of Religion* 22 (1983): 253-62; and Gary Bouma's "The Real Reason One Conservative Church Grew," *Review of Religious Research* 20 (1979): 127-37.

On growth through higher birthrates, see William McKinney and Wade Clark Roof, "Liberal Protestantism: A Socio-Demographic Perspective," in *Liberal Protestantism*, pp. 37-50.

As for growth through immigration, of the approximately 600,000 immigrants arriving in the United States annually, the majority (roughly 65 percent) have a Catholic religious identity (most of these coming from Latin America, the Caribbean, and the Philippines), but a significant minority are Pentecostal, fundamentalist, or evangelical. A majority of South Korean immigrants are Presbyterian and theologically conservative. My information on the religious character of the new immigrant population comes from a telephone interview with Father Silvano Tomasi, director of the Office of Migration, U.S. Catholic Conference, Washington, D.C., 23 October 1986.

Elites: The Leadership Factor

It is in the world of religious elites that polarization in the religious and political realms has become most crystallized. Though the tendencies toward political polarization among elites has been evident from the beginning of the twentieth century, it was not until the late 1950s and the early rumblings of the civil rights movement that these processes began to accelerate and become visible to a larger public. With each succeeding social issue in the next three decades—the war in Indochina, Third World poverty, women's rights, gay rights, abortion, the decline of the bourgeois family, nuclear energy and nuclear weaponry, global capitalism, and American policy in Central America—the separation seems to have grown wider.[27]

At both ends of the cultural axis elites have failed to bring along their constituencies effectively. As the two ends have polarized further, the elites have polarized furthest, leaving a substantial attitudinal gap between laity and leadership. That gap is evident not only in the content of various social and political values but also in the inclination of the religious leadership to translate those values into political action. Jeffrey Hadden was the first to make this observation for mainline Protestantism in his timely and insightful study *The Gathering Storm in the Churches*. At this point it is possible to extend his thesis to say that this gap also exists among conservatives. In brief, evangelical/fundamentalist elites tend to be further to the political right than their constituencies, while mainline elites tend to be further to the left than theirs. What is more, elites at both ends are much more prone to political activism than their constituencies want them to be.[28]

Though disparities exist among elites and laity within the main-

---

27. Among mainline elites there seems to be an increasing ideological uniformity particularly on the issues of capitalism, defense, and American foreign policy. Among evangelical elites there tends to be more variation. A political and social conservatism remains the dominant ideological commitment by far but a substantial minority are neither left nor right politically, and a significant and vocal minority are actively left of center.

28. See Harvey Cox, "The New Breed in American Churches: Sources of Social Activism in American Religion," *Daedelus* 96 (1967): 135-50; Rodney Stark, Bruce Foster, Charles Glock, and Harold Quinley, *Wayward Shepherds* (New York: Harper & Row, 1971); Harold Quinley, *The Prophetic Clergy* (New York: Wiley, 1974); and J. D. Hunter, "Religious Elites in Advanced Industrial Societies," *Comparative Studies in Society and History* 29 (1987): 360-74.

line and evangelical/fundamentalist wings, there is some evidence to suggest that these disparities are more pronounced within the mainline.[29] But why? For one thing, the gap between laity and clergy in social class and educational background appears to be greater in the mainline than in evangelical denominations. This is certainly true in the National Council of Churches, where, as Henry Pratt has shown, the elite are disproportionately drawn from a minority of the most liberal seminaries of the Northeast and delegates are disproportionately represented (72 percent as of 1966) by religious leaders with occupations similar to those held by the NCC executive staff (e.g., national and regional church executives, church publication editors, parachurch executives).[30] The local pastor tied to the concerns and interests of his/her parishioners is conspicuously underrepresented.[31] Second, the gap between abstract intellectual discourse and the discourse of everyday life seems to be greater in the mainline than in evangelical denominations. Liberal theology and progressive politics have never translated very well into a general populist ideology in the way that conservative theology and politics have. The intellectual circumlocutions they involve either require too much effort or are simply beyond the reach of average individuals who have given their lives over to the daily struggle to make ends meet. These average individuals are looking for moral formulae, even slogans, and liberal theology and politics are not easily given to these kinds of reductions. As long as the gaps created by modes of cultural discourse and by social class remain wide, the gap between laity and leadership, particularly within the mainline, will remain. More can be said on this count, but to do so one needs to refer to the demographics of religious leadership. Here, seminary enrollments provide a gauge.

Catholic leadership is facing a genuine crisis as the Catholic population continues to expand while the number of priests

---

29. See Hunter, Tucker, and Finkel, "Religious Elites and Political Values."

30. See Pratt, *The Liberalization of American Protestantism* (Detroit: Wayne State University Press, 1972); and "Organizational Stress and Adaptation to Changing Political Status: The Case of the National Council of Churches," in *The Church in Modern Society*, ed. Leo Martin (Los Angeles: Sage, 1977).

31. As Pratt suggests, "it is a reasonable inference that among NCC elites, the decline in the number of local pastors and laymen identified solely with a local congregation has been a factor in the waning conservatism of top NCC leaders" (*The Liberalization of American Protestantism*, p. 112).

diminishes. In 1964 Catholic seminary enrollment stood at 47,000, but by 1984 it had decreased to 12,000.[32] Protestantism fares well in comparison though not equally well in all denominations. In the progressivist wing of Protestantism, enrollments have held fairly even since 1960.[33] Between 1960 and 1972 there was roughly a 3 percent growth in mainline seminary enrollment, and between 1972 and 1985 there was a 19 percent increase. Evangelical seminaries have fared even better: enrollment increased 35 percent in the earlier period and 60 percent in the later period.

An increase in the number of women seminarians partly accounts for the stability and even growth in seminary enrollments in both factions of Protestantism. Of the traditionally male-dominated professions, this profession stands among the fastest growing for women. Between 1968 and 1976 the number of women in Protestant seminaries increased from 12 percent of total enrollment to 21 percent.[34] At present women constitute one-fourth (26 percent) of the total Protestant seminary enrollment nationally.[35] The percentage is slightly larger in mainline seminaries than in evangelical seminaries.[36] (Indeed, as a recent *New York Times* article reported, half of all seminarians at the Harvard Divinity School are women.)[37] In the

---

32. Ari Goldman, "Seminaries in U.S. Get a High Grade," *New York Times*, 5 October 1986, p. I, 27.

33. I base this statement on data found in the 1985-86 *Fact Book on Theological Education*, ed. William L. Baumgaertner (Vandalia, Ohio: Association of Theological Schools, 1986). The mainline seminaries included were Andover Newton, Boston University, University of Chicago Divinity, Duke, Episcopal Divinity School, Hartford, Harvard, Illif, Louisville, Lutheran (Philadelphia), Princeton, Union (New York), Virginia (Episcopal), and Yale/Berkeley. The evangelical seminaries were Asbury, Bethany, Bethel, Calvin, Conservative Baptist (Denver), Eastern Baptist, Fuller, Gordon-Conwell, Mid-Western Baptist, Nazarene, and Southern Baptist. These seminaries were chosen because of their prominence and because there were data for each going back to 1960.

34. This figure is derived from information taken from the U.S. Department of Health, Education and Welfare's *Digest of Educational Statistics* for 1970 (p. 70), 1974 (p. 80), and 1979 (p. 96).

35. See the 1985-86 *Fact Book on Theological Education*.

36. This is suggested by female enrollment in the seminaries of several mainline denominations. In the United Methodist seminaries, women constitute 29 percent of the total enrollment, in the Episcopal seminaries the figure is 34 percent, and in the United Church of Christ the figure is as high as 44 percent.

37. Ari Goldman, "As Call Comes, More Women Answer," *New York Times*, 19 October 1986, p. IV, 6.

more conservative theological seminaries their representation is only slightly less than the national average.[38]

The significance of the feminization of the clerisy for the future of Protestantism becomes plain when one recognizes that attitudinally, women seminarians are consistently further to the left (as a group) on moral, familial, and political issues than their male counterparts.[39] This is equally true among evangelical women seminarians.[40] This means that if demographic trends continue as they are or if they accelerate at all, there is a likelihood that the mainline elites may become even more entrenched in a left/liberal vision of religious and political leadership while the evangelical/fundamentalist elites may become even more diversified than they presently are. With regard to the leadership factor, women may possess the secret to the future.

Church Structure: The Organizational Factor

Institutional vitality is never vitality for its own sake but vitality in promoting a particular objective. When dealing with cultural institutions, one is interested in the effectiveness with which they defend and advance a particular moral vision. Mainline and evangelical Protestantism each emphasize their own institutional strategies for promoting their moral vision, and each is vigorous in its own way.

In the mainline the locus of institutional vitality resides in the official operations of the church structure itself. This is in large part born out of a tradition of religious administration that tends to be more episcopal or hierarchical in style—a tradition in which clergy and denominational bureaucrats assume the greatest responsibility

---

38. This is suggested by the enrollment figures for women in Southern Baptist seminaries—20 percent in 1985 (see the 1985-86 *Fact Book on Theological Education*, p. 87).

39. More evidence needs to be collected to establish this point certainly, but preliminary evidence can be found in *Women of the Cloth*, by Jackson W. Carroll, Barbara Hargrove, and Adair Lummis (San Francisco: Harper & Row, 1981). Data in the Connecticut Mutual Life survey "Values in the '80s" also suggest this.

40. The Evangelical Academy Project, which surveyed opinion among just under a thousand evangelical seminarians (among others), has provided very strong evidence of this. Female evangelical seminarians held more liberal views on virtually every social and political issue discussed—from the ERA to arms control (see Hunter, *Evangelicalism: The Coming Generation*).

for the life and identity of the church.[41] The vast wealth and power centralized within the structure of the major mainline denominations and transdenominations (the NCC and WCC in particular) dwarf those of their evangelical counterparts. The intensity of their public-sphere activity makes that of the conservative denominations seem insignificant. This in itself is laudatory. The problem is that the vastness and remoteness of the denominational authority in the mainline tends to militate against the involvement of the laity in denominational programs and, more importantly, against the programmatic initiatives of the laity. What is more, the political content and direction of many of the denominational programs makes them unattractive to a large number of the laity.[42] Such a gap is not nearly so great at the opposite end of the cultural axis.

The sectarian heritage and congregational style of religious administration more typical of the evangelical/fundamentalist churches together contribute to an environment that allows for a much greater involvement of the laity. Largely for this reason, the locus of institutional vitality (and ecumenical activity) within evangelicalism resides outside of the formal denominational structure and within the "unofficial" (denominationally independent), lay-dependent if not lay-initiated programs of the parachurch structure. Mainline Protestantism has its own parachurch network, of course, but nothing comparable to that of the evangelicals (see Table 3 on p. 41).

These data indicate the distribution of various kinds of parachurch organizations within different Protestant traditions. Unfortunately they do not provide any indication of the size of these organizations and, for that reason, they can only be suggestive. Even so, from Table 3 we can see that the principal focus of the mainline parachurch structure is on social welfare and social justice/civil liberties (mainly women's rights and gay rights organizations). If the number of organizations is any measure, the mainline gives relatively little priority to evangelism, the mass media, or publishing. Evangelicals have come to dominate these three areas of parachurch life, and three others as well—those concerned with the spiritual life of the Christian community, research and education, and international relief.

---

41. Many denominations in the mainline tradition are hierarchical for reasons of doctrine. Others whose official polity is congregational end up adopting a similar style of religious administration out of bureaucratic necessity (given their large memberships).

42. Thus, while the mainline leadership is busy being prophetic, the laity is actively being alienated.

Table 3
THE DISTRIBUTION OF VARIOUS INDEPENDENT PARACHURCH ORGANIZATIONS IN EVANGELICAL AND MAINLINE PROTESTANTISM

| | Protestant Tradition | |
	Evangelical (N = 361)	Mainline (N = 124)
Type of Parachurch Organization*		
Evangelistic	96%	4%
Spiritual Life	71	29
Social Welfare	41	59
International Relief	73	27
Justice/Civil Liberties	25	75
Research/Education	65	35
Publishing	71	29
Media/Arts	73	27
Professional	46	54

SOURCE: *The Directory of Religious Organizations in the United States* (Falls Church, Va.: McGrath, 1982).

As interesting as this might be, it does not give a feel for the real parachurch vitality. A few additional facts may help add some texture to this numerical canvas: (1) as of 1985, the 1,180 members and affiliated stations of the National Religious Broadcasters handled 85 percent of all Protestant religious broadcasting; (2) in 1980, the United States sent thirty thousand evangelical missionaries abroad—nearly eleven times the number of liberal Protestant missionaries; (3) since mid-century the number of periodicals affiliated with the Evangelical Press Association has grown to over three hundred, with an average net gain of twenty to twenty-five new periodicals per year; (4) in the same period, the number of evangelical publishing houses has grown to over seventy, and the number of evangelical bookstores marketing those books exceeds six thousand nationally; and (5) private evangelical primary and secondary schools have increased in number to roughly eighteen thousand, representing approximately two and a half million students.[43] The sociological significance of all of these activities is that they are all oriented toward expanding and deepening the reach of the evangel-

---

43. Figures and associated documentation can be found in the first chapter of Hunter's *Evangelicalism: The Coming Generation.*

ical moral vision to a larger number. This concern is notably lacking in the mainline by comparison.

It remains a question which end of the cultural axis has the more effective strategy for promulgating and defending its traditions. If the future of Protestantism depends on institutions requiring broad popular participation, the orthodox would seem to have an advantage. If it depends on a powerful, politicized, and cohesive elite, then the progressivists would seem to have an advantage.

Moral Energy: The Cultural Factor

By the "cultural factor" I mean the power of the moral vision of Protestantism to engender the commitment essential to its advancement, the kind of moral energy generated among adherents to press the cause forward. As we have already seen, on the whole the vision of the mainline generates little fervor at all except among those who articulate it and whose livelihoods derive from it. With few exceptions, the mainline laity remains socially and politically quietistic, aloof from the enthusiasms of its leadership.[44] Within conservative Protestantism, by comparison, a great deal of moral energy has been generated, particularly where its religious mission (evangelism, spirituality, world relief, etc.) is concerned. But what about the extent to which conservative Protestants are willing to advance their vision in the public square? How willing are they to politicize their vision? Alas, the problem of the Christian Right!

The literature on this subject is truly voluminous, and a few pages here will hardly do justice to its complexities. Yet a few observations are worth making. The first of these concerns the popular image of the New Christian Right. If one's view of reality is shaped at all by the mass media, one might have the image of conservative Protestantism as a growing monolith of crusaders who want to "bring into existence a kind of Christian Nazism (with the Bible as *Mein Kampf*)" in order to "goose-step mercilessly over the Godless."[45] If not Nazis, then Shi'ite fanatics. In a word, the moral energy appears to be high and very nearly out of control.

---

44. One exception would be the case of the Rev. Jesse Jackson, who in his 1984 bid for the presidency gained tremendous support from religiously liberal and conservative blacks in the primaries. See A. James Reichley, "Religion and the Future of American Politics," *Political Science Quarterly* 101 (1986): 23-47.

45. Walt Michalsky, "The Masquerade of Fundamentalism," *The Humanist* 41 (July/August 1981): 15-51.

Such characterizations are extreme, to be sure, but these and others like them abound. Nevertheless, they are all largely incorrect. For one thing, a large portion of the evangelical/fundamentalist population is just as aloof from the political engagement of its leadership as the mainline laity is from its leadership. A 1986 *L.A. Times* public opinion poll indicated that the majority of "white fundamentalists" disapproved of "clergymen who preach political views in their sermons." A slight majority also disapproved of "clergymen who work actively for the election of political candidates." As many disapproved as approved of "clergymen who run for public office" and a substantial minority even disapproved of "clergymen who take public stands on political issues." In all of these, the distribution of opinion among white fundamentalists differs only slightly from that of the larger population.

Indeed, a significant percentage of evangelicals/fundamentalists are openly embarrassed by if not hostile to the political programs and methods of the most publicly visible Christian Right groups, such as the Moral Majority/Liberty Federation, Pat Robertson, and the like. Public opinion polls consistently show only minority support for such groups and individuals, even among their alleged constituency. Deep disaffection from the programs and policies of the Christian Right is even greater among the orthodox intellectual elite—theologians, college faculty, seminarians, and the like.[46] In short, the Christian Right has been and will continue to be dismissed within its own community and especially by the evangelical literati, the opinion makers in the evangelical world.

Furthermore, there is no clear consensus among evangelicals/fundamentalists about how their interests as a community are reflected in particular issues. While generally conservative, evangelicals are deeply divided among themselves. The greatest consensus can be found on such family and personal morality issues as school prayer, pornography, homosexuality, and abortion. But when dealing with a wide range of public policy issues relating to the economy, welfare policy, and foreign affairs, the views of conservative Protestants are little different from other Americans. There are pointed differences between black and white evangelicals on these issues, but even among whites generally there are deep ideological divisions. All of this is to say that conservative Protestants as a

---

46. See J. D. Hunter, "Religion and Political Civility: The Coming Generation in American Evangelicalism," *Journal for the Scientific Study of Religion*, December 1984; and *Evangelicalism: The Coming Generation*.

group have not come to any collective determination of what their public interests are.

All of this suggests that the moral fervor behind the New Christian Right and thus much of its power have been grossly overestimated. By saying this, however, I do not intend to dismiss either their potential power or actual accomplishments. It is true, for example, that the evangelical/fundamentalist contingent of Protestantism is disproportionately conservative in its political leanings (and particularly over such issues as abortion, pornography, homosexuality, and the like). It is also true that the Religious Right has been sufficiently mobilized to register many new voters—two million in the 1984 elections[47]—and has succeeded in influencing a small number of local and regional elections. And it is true that its command over the electronic media and its mastery of the technology of mass mailings will always loom in the background as a potentially significant device for galvanizing large-scale popular support. Nevertheless, if the Religious Right has political muscle, it has not tested its capacity—and neither is it clear that it ever would or even could. At this point the greatest power of the Religious Right derives not from broadly based and deeply felt moral commitment but from the fear on the part of its opponents that it might have power. Perhaps the most optimistic assessment of the aspirations of the Religious Right is that it will achieve success through failure. Though it may fail in gaining any real power for itself, its vocal and persistent complaints may permanently alter the terms of (domestic) political debate in American life.

If the orthodox wing of Protestantism fails to coalesce into something akin to a Baptist Jihad, it may be because the moral energy it possesses may not be all it is reputed to be. If this is true, it may be because the theologically conservative are also involved in a process of resymbolizing the "historic faith" because their culture has succumbed to the modern imperatives of analysis, reflection, and introspection, in the process of which much of the inner imperative of their faith may have been lost.[48]

The Reorganization of the Public Square

Trends in the four interrelated factors we have just considered are all

---

47. See Reichley, "Religion and the Future of American Politics."
48. For more on this, see chapters 6 and 8 of Hunter's *Evangelicalism: The Coming Generation.*

important in projecting the future of American Protestantism. In the final analysis, however, they may prove relatively inconsequential in the light of still another factor—the changing composition of the public square. Extremists on both sides imply, in their rhetoric and actions, a passion to dominate the public square while maintaining a facade of pluralistic toleration. It remains to be seen whether it will be possible to establish a legal and political apparatus that can accommodate present conditions and sustain a genuine and peaceable pluralism. In any case, the current war of dogmas may not favor such a constructive armistice. The sociological impulse is for one to subjugate the other.

How the public square is restructured will in part be determined through litigation and legislation. Public education has already become an important arena for litigation of this sort, and it may become the central arena. The Hawkins County, Tennessee, and Mobile, Alabama, lawsuits are only the most recent examples. According to one study, these are just two of 130 formal initiatives nationwide in 1985 and 1986 concerning the moral content of public school curricula.[49] Most of these only have local significance (such as a complaint to a school board or public library commission). Several others involve state legislatures, federal courts, and the like. Whether local or national, their total number reportedly represents a 35 percent increase of such complaints over the previous year and a 117 percent increase over the year 1981-82. Other arenas of moral litigation and legislation include the the issue of displaying religious symbols on public property, matters of religious communication and protest (defined as a freedom-of-speech issue), abortion rights, and gay rights.[50]

---

49. These figures come from a study entitled "Attacks on the Freedom to Learn: A 1985-1986 Report," published by the People for the American Way.

50. Examples of cases now pending on the issue of religious symbols on public property include *Libin v. Town of Greenwich,* in which Connecticut volunteer firefighters were ordered to remove a cross from a traditional fire station Christmas display, and *Richmond Church of the Redeemer v. Henrico County, Va.* in which the church sued the county over its policy prohibiting religious activities in county facilities.

Cases involving free speech issues include *David Harley et al. v. Oregon State University,* in which university officials denied a student group permission to post prolife signs in a campus area used by other student groups for free speech purposes; *Stewart v. D.C. Armory Board,* in which a lay evangelist has sued for being prohibited from hanging "John 3:16" signs during a Redskins game at RFK stadium; *Thompson v. Waynesboro County School District,* in which students sued the school dis-

The results of this litigation may depend on the changing character of the nation's judges. President Reagan has already made over a third of all appointments to the federal judiciary, and by the time his second term is over, it is conceivable that he will have appointed over half.[51] Many if not most of these will be sympathetic to conservative judicial aims. Changes in the makeup of the Supreme Court may augment this trend.

The ways in which the public square is restructured will also be greatly determined by the coalitions of interests that form there. As we have already noted, partnerships among conservative Protestants, Catholics, and Jews on the one hand, and liberal Protestants, Catholics, and Jews on the other constitute a significant part of this coalition building. Even more important are the alliances these different religious coalitions form with larger, more diffuse, and secular interests—interests that mirror polarities in the larger religious community. For the religiously orthodox, these will be with the powerful interests and institutions of the old economic establishment; for the religiously progressivist, they will be with the formidable interests and institutions of the expanding secular cultural establishment. It is at this level that we see the class dimensions of a larger cultural conflict that has drawn the attention of numerous observers, a competition between the old business class versus the knowledge class.[52]

---

trict after being suspended for distributing a religious newspaper in the school building; and *Higgins v. Venice Area Middle School*, in which a Florida sixth grader sued school officials who confiscated New Testaments she gave out after her book report on the Bible.

Cases involving abortion rights issues include *Tacoma Stands Up for Life v. Federal Way Family Physicians* and *Pursley v. Fayetteville*, in which prolifers have challenged injunctions banning picketing in front of an abortion clinic; *Johnson v. Women's Health Organization*, in which a Delaware abortion clinic is being sued for malicious prosecution for causing the arrest of prolife reporters; and *Chattanooga Women's Clinic v. Martino*, in which an abortion clinic in Tennessee is suing prolifers for picketing in front of the clinic.

The most famous of the gay rights cases is *Bowers v. Hardwick*, in which the Supreme Court ruled that homosexual sodomy is not a fundamental right protected by the Constitution.

51. See Howard Kurtz, "The ABA Judges Screening Panel Criticized," *Washington Post*, 24 December 1985, p. A13; and "Reagan Transforms the Federal Judiciary," *Washington Post*, 31 March 1985, p. A1.

52. Alvin Gouldner, *The Future of Intellectuals and the Rise of the New Class* (New York: Oxford University Press, 1979); Berger, "American Religion: Conservative Upsurge, Liberal Prospects"; and *The New Class?* ed. B. Bruce Briggs (New Brunswick, N.J.: Transaction, 1979).

The fact that this cultural conflict is rooted in different social classes raises several questions. How tentative or cohesive are the linkages among these two classes and their religious counterparts? How do the two classes express their collective interests, and what kinds of strategic capabilities do they possess? Finally, how coherently and forcefully are their different class interests promoted?

It is impossible to answer these questions with any empirical specificity here. My own sense is that the ideological affinity and programmatic partnership between the religious mainline and the secular cultural establishment is much more consequential than that of their opposition because of the knowledge class's strategic (though not by any means total) domination of the means and mode of cultural production in American life. The power to define such things as the rules of public discourse and the legitimacy of different participants in the public square has always been linked to political power. The secular cultural establishment will, therefore, wield tremendous political power by definition. Because this occupational sector is expanding, its power is likely to expand concomitantly. As long as the interests of the religious mainline and the secular cultural establishment continue to coalesce and their ideology remains relatively cohesive, their political fortunes will be inextricably linked and invariably augmented.

How the public square is restructured may finally have something to do with historical momentum. Does the current conservative backlash represent a "rally in a bear market," as Benton Johnson once put it, or the beginnings of a conservative bull market? Put more precisely, will the *public ethos* of advanced capitalist societies be "reenchanted" or will it continue to follow the course of disenchantment. In a global perspective (that is, in light of the experience of other advanced industrial societies), the momentum favors the latter rather than the former. This momentum is grounded in the expanding power and autonomy of the secular state, the growth of the secular cultural establishment, and the exposure of an increasing portion of the population to the secularizing effects of higher education, whether in sectarian or nonsectarian institutions.

LOOKING TOWARD THE FUTURE

The future of American Protestantism hinges in part on the struggle among Protestants themselves to define their own future. This struggle is shaped by the kinds of power and resources each side has access to. How the future takes shape, then, depends on political considerations internal to Protestantism. But these dynamics cannot be understood alone. They are linked intimately with structural, political, and cultural dynamics that extend far beyond Protestantism—dynamics that may ultimately eclipse the significance of those intramural factors.

Even so, for Protestants themselves, the struggle to carve out their future is also a struggle to define the mission of the church. On this point the perspective offered here differs (respectfully) from that of *The Naked Public Square*. From the sociological vantage point, the religious mainline has not so much failed in its role of offering a culturally formative religion (articulating a public framework of moral reference). It continues to view culture formation as perhaps its chief mission. What has changed for the mainline is the meaning and direction of that task. It is over this that various factions within Protestantism contend. In all likelihood, however, if there is to be a resolution, it will be marked by some form of compromise. But which side would be favored in such a compromise? This may be the real question.

In sum, it hardly needs saying that what happens within Protestantism is of tremendous significance. For one thing, it is in this religious tradition that we find perhaps the original location of this larger cultural division—the seeds of the larger cultural realignment. The cultural polarities described here, of course, now extend far beyond this faith. Nevertheless, Protestantism may continue to be its most compelling metaphor, for it is in Protestantism that the dynamics of cultural realignment are perhaps most clearly articulated and carefully organized. In the end the future of Protestantism may contain (if only by analogy) the future of American cultural life itself.

Continuity and Change in Mainline Protestantism

Thomas Sieger Derr

I have not yet recovered from my surprise at being asked to write this essay, believing that it belongs more properly to an American church historian such as Martin Marty or Robert Handy. I do indeed have a deep interest in these matters, but beyond interest I suspect my principal qualifications for writing this are biographical: I am a born and bred Protestant "mainliner" (the United Church of Christ), educated at a mainline seminary (Union in New York) in the heyday of neo-orthodoxy, an activist veteran of the civil rights movement, and a perennial participant in the ecumenical movement. So I would seem to fit the profile required for this task, someone intuitively sympathetic to the mainline churches. And I am.

But despite what their critics say, these churches, even their leaders, are quite diverse, and no one can typify them, much less speak for them. Besides, biography can be deceptive. I would describe myself almost exactly as Richard Neuhaus describes *himself*[1]—a Christian who is catholic and ecumenical, economically pragmatic, culturally conservative, and a political centrist—which similarity obviously does not mean that we always come to the same conclusions! For example I use the word *liberal* as a politically centrist term, a point I would be glad to defend on another occasion. For now I will only state the obvious, that although I am clearly sympathetic to the mainline churches and their leaders, I cannot claim to represent their views here. I offer only a personal reflection, informed as it doubtless is by my natural sympathies.

---

1. See Neuhaus, *The Naked Public Square* (Grand Rapids: Eerdmans, 1984), pp. vii-viii.

WHENCE THE MAINLINE?

It is not easy to define what we mean by "mainline Protestant," though we can probably get rather quickly a sufficiently adequate idea to proceed. One simple system is just to equate the term with membership in the National and World Councils of Churches. Probably all American churches we would want to include as mainline fit this criterion, but then we would have to argue whether all who hold such ecumenical memberships are really what we mean by "mainline"—for instance, several black denominations. It is also customary to say that the mainline churches are, besides ecumenical, also "liberal" theologically and socially. But that is only a relative term, meaning at best more liberal than the evangelicals, and papering over a multitude of exceptions and qualifications.

So we introduce further refinements, historical and cultural in nature. To be "mainline" a church must have been, or have in the twentieth century become, representative of a certain attitude, claiming to speak to or for the nation, embodying a public religion with intended consequences for the whole of American culture, its leaders linked by class and education with elites in other fields. These are somewhat amorphous conditions, however, and difficult to pin down. All other attempts at precise definition failing, we can always resort simply to listing those churches that meet our criteria (whatever they really are). But we would not necessarily be able to agree on a definitve list. Nearly everyone would include the two major ecumenical Lutheran bodies, for example, but Richard Neuhaus does not, even denying them the term "Protestant," which is one of the minor mysteries of his book *The Naked Public Square*. (Surely if anyone has a claim to be called Protestant, it is the Lutherans.) So not even a convincing list of names can be produced.

But if we cannot be precise, we can come close enough to forge ahead. So let us abandon the definitional task at this point and address ourselves to the main problem, which is, of course, the current difficulties of these churches. Usually statistics are cited to tell the story: declining membership, declining church school enrollments, reduced budgets, and a rising average age of membership all lead to reduced public influence. Extrapolation of trends would yield the conclusion that, despite the evanescent revival of the fifties, these churches will eventually disappear as a distinctively Christian presence in America. Aiding the decline is a vigorous push from the renascent evangelical movement, attracting members away from the mainline and even appearing within the mainline churches to challenge their direction. All around is a rising tide of new religious forms diluting the once-dominant influence of the mainline churches, reducing them to one group among many, a minority with its own pejorative label, WASP—though they are ethnically pretty mixed, and many of their challengers, notably the evangelical grouping, are just about as WASPish.

People who have some acquaintance with the history of American religion will have a few caveats. The statistical decline looks worse when compared with the fifties, the high point of religious allegiance. The low point was probably the time of the American Revolution, and there has been a noticeable rhythm of renewal and decline ever since. No religious situation is static. Viewed in long-term context, the current decline is not remarkable, nor is the emergence of new religious forces. Extrapolation as a predictor is here, as it often is, methodologically silly. Some of the newly strong religious forms, moreover, would seem to be continuing many of the characteristics of the mainline, such as its liberal political bent—the black churches, for example. It is also probable that the degree of switching membership from mainline to evangelical churches has been exaggerated.[2]

Nevertheless, the caveats having been duly noted, there has still been a measurable decline, and those of us who care about this tradition are worried. Recent statistics claiming to show that the membership drop has "bottomed out" are cold comfort to us, whistling in the dark. We look about, as our forebears did in periods of *their* decline, to find the causes, hoping we may do something to bring about renewal once again. Almost at once we face the charge that the root cause of the difficulty is liberalism—liberalism in theology and social policy. The mainline, it is said by its critics, has abandoned its evangelical heritage and is now paying the price for its apostasy. Once, and even from its American beginnings in the seventeenth century, it had a vision of a religious vocation for America, the new locus of the drama of salvation, the redeemer nation. It would be a *Christian* America with an evangelical mission to be a light to the nations. But now in the twentieth century the religious mainline that had borne that vocation and that vision has abandoned it all to a relativistic, pluralistic view of the nation. Now the mainline says that the nation was never simply a "Christian" America. Now it rejects the notion that America had a special place in the divine economy, that it was "chosen." The new evangelicals have ac-

---

2. See Grant Wacker, "Uneasy in Zion: Evangelicals in Postmodern Society," in *Evangelicalism and Modern America*, ed. George Marsden (Grand Rapids: Eerdmans, 1984), pp. 183n.4.

cordingly arisen (or been raised up) to claim this abandoned heritage for themselves.

Now there is much truth in this charge, let us not deny it. It has prima facie plausibility. Up through the nineteenth century American mainline Protestantism was indeed dominated by the vision of a thoroughly Christianized America and spurred on by the conviction that God in his providence meant it to be so. The great times of renewal in American religious history manifested this pervasive belief. The "Second Awakening" in the first part of the nineteenth century offers an especially vivid example. The promise of newly won American independence was also perilous, as church leaders had to own up to their traditional claims to be in the forefront of God's redeeming activity in history, responsible at last for their own national destiny without any colonial dependence on the mother country. The newly opened trans-Appalachian frontier presented both opportunity and danger, growing space for the new nation to be sure, but also an uncivilized land whose barbarism might corrupt the whole republic. The answer was clear: missions that would at once Christianize and civilize the new territories. Indeed, the two goals were viewed as one, and that is the point. There was no suggestion of a secular society. Sermons easily linking irreligion with decadence assumed the connection between religion and high culture, between church and civil polity.

To this end—Christian civilization—the constitutional disestablishment of religion presented no bar. To be sure, there were doubters who clung to the received wisdom of the ages, that a healthy society requires a national church, or at least some official support of religion. But, disestablishment having become inevitable fact, doubts gave way to resolution and finally to optimism, as mainline leaders forged a series of cooperative associations backed by private contributions, anticipating the transformation of the nation into, shall we say, the apple of God's eye. One can see the metamorphosis in the biography of Lyman Beecher, for example, who at first trembled for the fate of civilization should the establishment fall, but then in the end became the champion of voluntarism, the leading architect of the "benevolent empire."

From this enterprise there flowed a continuing stream of ambitious projects, driven by the energy of religious revival and millennial confidence in advancing the kingdom of God. The link between revivalism and social reform has been well documented. Movements for temperance, aboliton of slavery, world peace, prison reform, advancement of education—all were fueled by the evangelical vision of an America transformed into the perfect Christian commonwealth. A burgeoning foreign missionary enterprise was meant to export this religious civilization for the salvation of other lands also. At the end of the century the Social Gospel movement, despite its self-conscious distance from much evangelical piety of the time and its different emphasis on economic justice and urban renewal, arose nevertheless within the mainstream and shared its vision of a transformed society to herald the coming kingdom of God.

For most of the century this mainstream ecumenical project was undergirded by a de facto theological unity of the Calvinist and Pietist traditions, representatives of which together found themselves, despite their differences, "orthodox" and firmly opposed to the rationalist tradition, which they considered not only heretical but inadequate to sustain the morality required by Christian civilization. This was the evangelical front built and vigorously defended by the likes of Charles G. Finney, the leading revivalist of the mid-century.

Theological liberalism entered in force toward the end of the century and is alleged by critics to be a key element in the mainstream's fall from grace. In addition, the mainline churches, having been so long a dominant cultural force and having so habitually identified the welfare of their churches with the welfare of the nation, gradually began to lose the perspective of transcendence and to concentrate primarily on the fortunes of America, a fate to which their liberal this-worldly theology inclined them. Having become followers of the nation's secular health, they eventually lost their distinctively Christian voice, and with it their vision of a Christian commonwealth preparing for the coming kingdom of God.

Now in our day it is the contemporary evangelicals who have recovered not only the old honored "evangelical" label of the mainstream but likewise the dream of America as God's country. They even pursue their goal much as the old mainline did, through voluntary societies and private contributions, their Wycliffe Bible Translators and World Vision International and Intervarsity Urbana missionary rallies all having earlier counterparts among the mainliners. Their theology, too (excepting that of the fundamentalists and, if they are also evangelicals, that of the Pentecostalists), is not that much different. All things considered, it does indeed seem as though the historic mantle were theirs for the claiming.

Of course the picture is not quite that neat. There were dark spots in the old vision that ought not to be reborn, such as the danger of idolatrous nationalism or race pride and blindness toward the experience of black Americans, with their understandably pessimistic assessment of the prospects for a Christian America. It would be comforting to report that the contemporary evangelical resurgence has corrected these imperfections, but such a report would be premature. I would not want to defend the gospel faithfulness in these matters of either the old or the new evangelicalism. As many commentators have noted, the new evangelicals are becoming in many ways as culture-accommodating as the mainline forces they seek to displace.

I also question, of course, that simple summary of American theological history—that the mainline has become apostate liberal and the evangelicals are faithful to authentic Christianity. I sometimes read of the theology of mainline churches, or at least of their leaders, that they are not only liberal but captive to scientific rationalism, even skeptical about the transcendent. The evangelical liberals of the nineteenth century certainly did not fit this description, and I seriously doubt that it applies to their twentieth-century descendents. Furthermore, I wonder how many would even call themselves liberal. The leadership generation was brought up under the sway of neo-orthodoxy, the influence of which, it seems to me, is far too quickly dismissed by many of the mainline's critics, especially those with an interest in painting them as "liberal" in order to condemn them. Like many of my generation in mainline American Protestantism, I recall the glee with which I first heard Richard Niebuhr's caustic dismissal of liberalism as the movement in which "a God without wrath brought men without sin into a Kingdom without judgment through the ministrations of a Christ without a cross."[3] This was meat and drink to us. Those who have written us off as theological liberals either have too narrow a view of what orthodoxy requires or have overrated the effect of the sixties.

Nor is it entirely accurate to characterize current evangelicalism as the old faith recovered in its purity. Much of it is a distinctly modern creation born of a reaction to modernism. It is situationally constituted, so much so that some of *its* critics have seen it as an attempt (and a futile attempt at that) to fight the uncertainties of this century with nostalgia for the last one. It is determined by the *current* cultural situation and is not necessarily the bearer of timeless Christian truth. Like liberal theology, it is one attempt to adjust to a changing world. If that is so, then what is at issue between these two camps is not really the content of Christian theology conceived objectively, propositionally, but the style of faithfulness. Acknowledging that

---

3. Niebuhr, *The Kingdom of God in America*, 2d ed. (New York: Harper & Row, 1959), p. 193.

both groups are adaptations to the modern world, the question is which has brought the Christian faith more meaningfully, more authentically to our situation today. If we put the question that way, we may at least entertain the idea that the mainline has still a powerful and truly Christian word to say and that its demise is nowhere in sight after all. For the moment this is only a suggestion, but I will shortly work at putting some flesh on its bones.

Meanwhile let me take a closer look at the charge against the mainline I just mentioned, a charge at least as serious as its alleged theological apostasy—namely, that it has lost its transcendent perspective and become a mere camp follower of secular society. Certainly the developed liberalism of the twenties had let itself become overly accommodated to American culture, optimistically universalizing then-dominant values, assuming that ours really was a Christian nation. Even the Social Gospelers, critics of the culture, saw a reformed America as their goal and dared to think that it would herald, and perhaps even *become* the kingdom of God. Neo-orthodoxy, of course, excoriated these pretensions in the name of divine transcendence.

But, say the contemporary foes of mainline Protestantism, the neo-orthodox protest faded, and the dominant liberalism reasserted itself with new vigor—and new pretensions—in the sixties, now more than ever identifying with contemporary values. This time it was the radical values then fashionable. The mainline denominations became indistinguishable from the political left, without any Christian voice of their own, mere echoes of the trendy radicals. Of course this was hardly the first time in American history such a charge had been made. Robert Handy cites one from 1866 in which the southern Methodist bishops accuse the northern Methodists of having "become incurably radical. They teach for doctrine the commandments of men. They preach another Gospel. They have incorporated social dogmas and political tests into their church creeds."[4] But we do not live long enough to experience what happened a century ago, and *our* sixties seemed a time of unique politicization in the churches. Thus the decade becomes the perfect example of accommodationist liberalism, and we begin to understand why the collapse of the sixties' utopian pretensions also saw the precipitous decline of the churches that had identified themselves with that species of cultural foolishness.

---

4. Handy, *A Christian America*, 2d ed. (New York: Oxford, 1984), p. 60.

One obvious problem with this analysis is that the radicals of the sixties did not speak for mainstream America, and thus going along with their extreme denunciations of American culture can hardly be called accommodationism. Church leaders who heard the call of radicalism were certainly not celebrating the dominant social values of their time. They were listening to a radical, alienated minority. How is this, if the crime of their liberalism is adapting Christianity to culture? It may be replied that the mode of operation is still accommodationist, but the leadership has now chosen to accommodate to the "new class," the information elite of which it feels itself part. But in that case its accommodationism still amounts to defiance of "middle America" and, seen against the larger cultural picture, is still a form of radicalism. It is clearly not the same as the culture identification of 1920s liberalism. Explaining both as liberal accommodationism is at least confusing, and probably wrong.

Perhaps, then, the troubles of mainline Protestantism are not attributable to liberal accommodationism after all, but, says an alternative hypothesis, to a split between the radical denominational leadership and the middle-American character of the laity. It was this internal dissension that dispirited the laity. Unable to wrest control of their churches from the bureaucrats because of the latter's manipulative cleverness, they began to drift away.

Dissension with the laity may have contributed to the current Protestant malaise, but it ought not to be exaggerated. The mainline denominations still have working forms of democratic accountability, far more than the independent evangelical organizations, and a leadership totally at odds with the laity cannot endure forever, even if bureaucratic entrenchment makes it hard to dislodge. These intrachurch quarrels may entertain or dismay us, and they do provide food for hostile critics who exaggerate them up to and beyond the point of prevarication (one thinks of the television program *60 Minutes* in its report on the National and World Councils of Churches, or of the *Readers Digest*'s regular assaults on the truth in its articles on the ecumenical bodies), but they are temporary and do not tell us much of the long-term problems. They may indeed tell us something about the proper role of prophets championing unpopular causes out of their own understanding of Christian faithfulness—a species that has regularly arisen in American Protestantism and that has an honored place in the tradition of Protestant preaching—but these are certainly not cultural accommodationists. And if culture religion is the problem of the mainline, radicalism in some of its leaders ought to be a bit of a welcome antidote.

Liberal theology and leftist politics are separate issues. It is not clear to me that they are causally related. Data that show a rough correlation between the two are papering over a raft of exceptions and qualifications and in any event do not demonstrate a cause-and-effect relationship. Liberal theology in the nineteenth century defended the Gospel of Wealth as well as the Social Gospel. In our time the antiliberal neo-orthodox movement was often to the left in politics, and there are plenty of politically liberal evangelicals. A Roper survey of theological faculty pointed out both their dominant political liberalism *and* their religious orthodoxy.[5]

So leftist politics among the mainline leadership (or for that matter among the Roman Catholic leadership) must have other sources than theology. In any event there is considerable diversity of political opinion covered by the term *left*. Someone who is economically liberal—a Catholic bishop for example—is not necessarily theologically liberal. A Protestant leader may easily be economically liberal, culturally conservative, and theologically centrist. One may, without inconsistency, hold the "liberal" position on abortion, a more "conservative" one on homosexuality, and find that neither correlates meaningfully with one's particular place on the theological spectrum. The picture is too mixed to be of much help in our analysis. To say it again, the political element would seem to be a relatively minor factor in the current problems of the mainline denominations.

My sense of the matter is that culture religion is a more basic issue. To use Leonard Sweet's formula, the churches, instead of setting standards for society, have set themselves to meet the needs of society.[6] In so doing they have lost their distinctively Christian identity and thrown away the basic reason that people come to them. Naturally it is easier to say this roundly than to spell out all its implications. The churches can hardly be indifferent to the needs of society; they would not be Christian if they were. But the point is to recover the being apart, the sense of transcendence that has recently been in eclipse.

Before I go on to sketch what I think is a viable future posture for the mainline, I want to acknowledge the presence of some other factors in their current weakness. I have been concentrating on the internal forces, what the churches have become and are doing that

---

5. See *This World*, Summer 1982, pp. 28ff.; and the comments of Michael Novak on p. 101.

6. Sweet, "The 1960s: The Crises of Liberal Christianity and the Public Emergence of Evangelicalism," in *Evangelicalism and Modern America*, p. 31.

puts them in their current fix. But of course they do not operate in a vacuum, and the impact of the larger culture has affected them in ways quite beyond their control. Already toward the end of the nineteenth century, that era now held up as the golden age of mainline influence on our culture, there were those who noticed that changing social forces, notably urbanism and industrialism, were pushing religion out of its favored place. A temporary resurgence of optimism after the First World War was followed by disillusion with the ideals of wartime, isolationism, and social unrest at home. It was a time of intellectual skepticism about religion, a period of widely advertised cynicism and private hedonism, the epoch of "flaming youth." Handy, quoting H. L. Mencken to the effect that "Protestantism in this great Christian realm is down with a wasting disease," says that "by the twenties, the force of a public conscience informed by religion was in fact diminishing."[7]

The period of uncertainty and disintegration produced its reaction, predictably. While the mainline pursued biblical criticism, social action, and the nascent ecumenical movement, conservatives arose to champion biblical inerrancy and American nationalism. It is not too much to claim that this division still marks us today, more than half a century later: on the one side complex theology, moral revisionism, liberal politics, and ecumenism, while on the other biblical literalism, propositional, catechetical theology, moral absolutism, religious patriotism, and a distrust of all internationalism from the United Nations to the World Council of Churches. Periods of cultural upheaval are hard on the establishment, on the mainline; and, as all cliche lovers know, this has been a tumultuous century. Except, perhaps, for the atypical fifties, there has been enough turmoil virtually to guarantee the strength of a movement devoted to affirming the verities of an earlier and more stable time. It has a perennial appeal to the disaffected. Whether it will prove a trustworthy guide to the future or speak to and for most Americans are other matters entirely.

I should also mention some smaller changes that have affected adversely the fortunes of the mainline churches. Demographic shifts have hurt some regionally strong churches in the areas of their concentration. The socio-economic status of the mainline membership has been rising, and this is a phenomenon usually correlated with lower birthrates and lower church membership. Both the privatized religion of the last decade and the increasing localism of American

---

7. Handy, *A Christian America,* p. 175.

life with its distrust of large structures have hurt the institutional life of the national denominations.[8]

Finally, in my summary sketch of the external factors impinging on the mainline, I come to the most important change of all: religious pluralism. More than anything else, the simple but powerful fact of diversity has brought about the decline of mainline Protestant hegemony. Of course one should not exaggerate the unity of the past. American religious diversity has occasioned some bitter quarrels at the very center of the establishment denominations. I think of the complaint of one mainline minister during the Great Awakening, speaking contemptuously of revivalist preaching:

> the want of knowledge in a teacher . . . may easily be made up and overbalanced by great zeal, and affecting tone of voice, and a perpetual motion of the tongue. If a speaker can keep his tongue running in an unremitting manner and can quote memoriter a large number of texts from within the covers of the Bible, it matters not to many of his hearers whether he speaks sense or nonsense.[9]

Our religious past probably seems more homogeneous to us than it did to those who lived it.

Nevertheless, by the mid-nineteenth century, at least, the record points to a rather remarkable unity of Protestant thought and action and a level of influence on American culture not achieved either before or since. Protestants then were conscious enough of their own differences, but they had learned to cooperate voluntarily for common goals, a moral consensus they assumed would find acceptance in public opinion and reinforcement in appropriate laws.

It was immigration more than anything else that spoiled their grand hopes, bringing such heterogeneity to the American religious map that a uniform Christian commonwealth was no longer thinkable. The public schools, once thoroughly Christianized and Protestantized, gradually became secular and assumed from the churches the task of education for citizenship with a lowest-common-denominator morality. Church-state conflicts multiplied as the religion clauses of the First Amendment became an issue, a striking twentieth-century phenomenon relatively rare (at least at the Su-

---

8. See Richard G. Hutcheson, Jr., *Mainline Churches and the Evangelicals: A Challenging Crisis?* (Atlanta: John Knox Press, 1981), pp. 110ff., 123-30, 157-58.

9. Noah Worcestor, quoted by Winthrop Hudson in *Religion in America* (New York: Scribner's, 1965), p. 116.

preme Court level) in the days of Protestant hegemony. Religious events, even large revivals, lost their community-wide character and were confined to the now specialized world of the churches. In short, the special identity of mainline Protestantism with American culture was over. The mainline had been relativized, its influence diluted.

The superficial revival of the fifties was possible at least partly because at the level of folk religion very different confessions responded similarly to cultural impulses. The Rev. Norman Vincent Peale, the Rev. Billy Graham, Monsignor (later Bishop) Fulton J. Sheen, and Rabbi Joshua Loth Liebman all wrote *(mutatis mutandis)* the same popular book. And such ad hoc confluences are still possible. But diversity is the brute reality. Any program for a public ethic religious in character and expression must account for this new reality and not expect to resurrect the nineteenth-century ideal.

This is not to say that the new situation is thoroughly secular. It is religiously pluralistic and only rather spottily secular. There are surveys aplenty to show the enduring religiosity of the American people. Part of the genius of the humorist Garrison Keillor is to joke about religion in a respectful way that takes for granted that it really matters in the lives of ordinary people. Richard Neuhaus has pointed out that we regularly invoke moral language in public debate, displaying our allegiance to the idea of normative truth. We believe in virtue in public life. We compromise as a matter of expediency, not because we believe no matter of truth is at issue.[10]

There is some disagreement, to put it mildly, as to whether our persistent religious sentiments are sufficiently recognized by the prevailing powers. There are those, for example, who fault the Supreme Court for secularizing our institutions beyond the intent of the Founders and beyond endurance; and there are those, like myself, who read the Court's record as having rejected the hostile "wall of separation" concept in favor of a benevolent neutrality toward religion that Madison would have approved. There are those who believe that mainline Protestantism has capitulated to the secularizers and acquiesced in the marginalization of religion; and there are those, like myself, who believe it has tried to adjust to the new pluralism in good faith, although obviously with mixed success. Its task is not to go back a hundred years but to witness to its Christian heritage in ways appropriate to this nation in this century, a culture in

---

10. Neuhaus, *The Naked Public Square*, p. 111.

which religion has lost its privileged place and become, in Martin Marty's neat summary word, "escapable."[11]

WHITHER THE MAINLINE?

The first step in trying to find a viable, appropriate course for mainline Protestantism is to come to terms with the dilemma of prophetism and popularity, of transcendent criticism and cultural affirmation. Some of the mainline's critics accuse it of both these faults without, I think, having resolved the inconsistency in their attacks. On the one hand these churches, or at least their leaders, are accused almost gleefully of alienating the rank and file (and the rest of the general public too) with their radical politics, "churning out" prophetic pronouncements that reflect their intellectually elitist class bias more than real Christian perception. Lacking principled integrity, they defend an active state, involved in all areas of life, not because of their theological convictions but because it suits their interest as bureaucrats. No wonder they are losing members, a fate they richly deserve for being out of step with the laity and negative about America.

On the other hand the opposite is also said, and sometimes by the same people: the heritage of liberal theology is cultural conformism, and the mainline churches, basically liberal, have accordingly lost their transcendent perspective and thus their Christian authenticity. Accustomed to being cultural leaders, close to power and influence, and bearing a long tradition of identifying America's fortunes with the divine purposes in history, they have become captive to the national ethos, in effect idolaters. Sensing that there is nothing particularly distinctive about such churches, the laity drift away to other pursuits, or they join more conservative churches that give them a sense of belonging more particular and more meaningful than the formless culture in which their daily lives are set.

These two positions are rife with contradiction. Are mainline churches weak because they attack the culture or because they bless it? Are they too radical or too conformist? Are numbers a sign of strength, an indication that a church is meeting people's needs? Or are they a sign of weakness, an indication that a church has sought prosperity at the expense of faithfulness to the gospel? Possibly one should have some sympathy for the critical confusion, as the prob-

---

11. Marty, *A Nation of Behavers* (Chicago: University of Chicago, 1976), p. 23.

lem here is ancient. Every national church has faced it. How can a church speak meaningfully to the real daily lives of its people without compromising the gospel? Must a church become a sect to retain its purity? It is a dilemma familiar to all of us.

The mainline, too, has lived out this tension in its own recent history. I refer again to the neo-orthodox movement, which arose in reaction to the liberal complacency of the twenties. "The church, tied to the culture which it sponsored, suffers corruption with it," wrote Richard Niebuhr in 1935. "Only a new withdrawal followed by a new aggression can then save the church and restore to it the salt with which to savor society . . . . The task of the present generation appears to lie in the liberation of the church from its bondage to a corrupt civilization."[12] We see in retrospect that that was an appropriate judgment for the time, though it was not obvious to everyone when it was written. Perhaps the only answer to the dilemma of cultural affirmation and transcendence is a rhythmic alteration, the pattern of which depends on the difficult art of discerning aright the signs of the times.

Not that the mainline is failing to criticize the nation right now. American foreign policy continues to be subject to withering attack from the mainline social action people, and ironically it is the evangelicals who have become culture-affirming, as inoffensive as accommodationist liberals ever were. If the hypothesis that uncritical celebration of the culture leads eventually to decline is correct, then it is the evangelicals who should soon begin to hurt, while the mainline shows signs of recovering its transcendent voice, continuing the neo-orthodox protest. This assessment has the merit of according with the self-understanding of the mainline leadership, which sees itself as closer to the role of culture critic than cheerleader.

However they manage the role, it does seem clear that the mainline churches must in the future maintain their activism. That would head my short list of characteristics they must have in order to be faithful to their heritage—indeed, to be authentically Christian. They have a three-centuries-long tradition of commitment to public discourse. Their religion has never been merely private belief. They have always claimed a role in shaping America's course, always spoken to the national destiny. Theirs has been, in their own eyes, a responsible participation, done out of love for America, speaking critically not merely to denounce but to call the nation to righteousness.

---

12. Niebuhr, quoted by Handy in *A Christian America*, p. 183.

It would be out of character, absurd, and a crying shame for the churches to abandon this public role and retreat to the quest for other-worldly salvation. They cannot even settle for the kind of limited social action that wages war only on individual vices—abuse of alcohol and other drugs, pornography, aberrant sexual mores. That is neither a credible nor a desirable future for the mainline, and we all know it. This is a public tradition. It will not willingly seek marginalization and dismissal by the world. On the other hand, I do not know that we—mainliners—should seek to perpetuate the kind of preoccupation with relevance expressed in that World Council slogan "The world sets the agenda for the church." We have come through a fascination for the secular so entrancing that at times we forgot we were called Christians. We have to begin with our faith—but then we have to move out to the world. We cannot baptize the secular uncritically, but neither can we reject its significance or fail to see in it God's world in need of our ministry.

If the commitment to activism is clear, the form it should take is not. If we reject the "two kingdoms" error and decline the sectarian perfectionist withdrawal, we must be prepared to bend and turn, to compromise with the world while yet keeping our Christian integrity. Many in the mainline tradition work this out in political involvement, progressive and reformist. Others believe that this course is too likely to make the church captive to a political faction, and they have preferred the more traditionally religious role of the prophet. Prophets have an honored place in the history of the American mainline—abolitionists, civil rights marchers, peace activists, inner city crusaders for economic justice, and so on, people who have found progressive political action inadequate and chosen instead to confront evils head on. Critics who scorn the would-be prophetic statements of (as they call them) the "social action curia" should remember some of this history, such as the Federal Council of Churches' declaration shortly after the First World War that racial segregation was "undesirable and a violation of the Gospel of love and human brotherhood" and that the Council would pledge itself to "work for a non-segregated Church and a non-segregated society."[13]

Of course prophets can also be wrong, fully justifying the scorn of their critics. The history of American prophecy is littered with failed causes, such as the Sabbath-observance and temperance

---

13. Federal Council of Churches declaration, quoted by Handy in *A Christian America*, p. 173.

crusades. The nineteenth-century guardians of American righteousness could not agree on the moral issue of slavery or on whose
arms God was blessing in the Civil War. But the prophetic tradition
endures, and fortunately so. If the churches did not take on that role,
if they did not engage themselves on behalf of those who are hurt
and powerless in our national life, they would scarcely deserve to be
called Christian churches.

I might say, parenthetically as it were, a word about the so-called
"civil religion," which defenders such as Robert Bellah and Sidney
Mead consider a viable means for expressing transcendence. Bellah
has argued that "the American civil religion is not the worship of the
American nation but an understanding of the American experience
in the light of ultimate and universal reality."[14] It is available as an
ideal to challenge the reality of America, and thus not in danger of
becoming mere culture religion.

I suppose we might all agree that at the very least the presence of
civil religion is an acknowledgment of the ancient wisdom that civil
law and public virtue must be grounded in normative, transcendent
truth. But I would guess that very few of the mainline church
leaders would find it an adequate religious expression. For one
thing, the odor of hypocrisy clings to it. Lacking any anchor in the
popular mind, it looks like an invention concocted to substitute for
the real, living faiths that have been constitutionally disestablished.
More seriously and dangerously, civil religion invites national
idolatry, effectively cutting off all criticsm of the nation's purposes
and all moral criticism of its actions.[15] Church leaders prefer to
speak instead out of their own authentic historic faith, independent
of the state.

Since I am being prescriptive in this section, I will say that the
mainline churches ought to continue their historic habit of contributing to and helping to maintain a public ethic, a tradition of
civic virtue, not by acquiescing in the substitute of civil religion but
by speaking frankly out of real, living Christian faith. There is no
need to pretend that they have lost their religious identity or that
speaking in that identity they have nothing to say to a religiously
polyglot nation. The situation of pluralism requires not religious

14. Bellah, "Civil Religion in America," in *Religion in America*, ed.
William G. McLoughlin and Robert N. Bellah (Boston: Beacon Press,
1968), p. 20.
15. I have developed these arguments in *Church, State, and Politics*,
which I wrote with A. E. Dick Howard and John W. Baker (Washington:
American Trial Lawyers Foundation, 1981), pp. 84-86.

silence or an artificial, least-common-denominator faith but honest, authentic contributions from actual religious communities—with all the "sectarianism" that Jefferson wanted kept *out* of the public debate.

To be sure, this is easier said than done. Religious convictions are ultimate convictions, not easily susceptible to the kind of practical compromise a pluralistic democracy requires. In practice even the firmest moral convictions of a church may not find sufficient support in the body politic to gain the force of law. Religious people will have to settle often for less than the ultimates in which they believe, and they will often be bitter about that, as the current abortion debate demonstrates. The *practical* result of religious debate on public issues may after all be something like a vague moral consensus with a lot of gaps.

But far better to have real religious voices in the debate than to pretend that honest religion has nothing to say to our national life, denying it access to the public forum as irrelevant at best and dangerously disruptive at worst. This is the main point of Richard Neuhaus's *Naked Public Square*, and I fully agree with it. We cannot simply abandon our religiously grounded moral claims as if they were mere preferences. We cannot pretend we are not religious when we are, or that our religion touches only parts of our life when it shapes the whole. If our public ethic is not shaped by an active religious presence, it hides the true nature of the values of most Americans. Such an ethic is false, and a commonwealth built on it cannot claim to be truly a democracy, because it is refusing to listen to some of its most important voices.

Whether or not Neuhaus is right (and he may be) in his further point that the absence of genuine transcendent religion in the public square would eventually lead to totalitarianism,[16] I think we can at least agree that many of the values we are most anxious to defend against the omnicompetent state—the preservation of human rights, for example—are securely protected only by a real religious presence. And such a presence can be effective only if it is institutional—religious communities, churches, with the power to teach their heritage to the next generation. Again we see the role I would wish for the mainline churches: an autonomous community sprung from Christian faith, speaking to the state openly and unashamedly out of its religous convictions, yet with real sympathy for the mission of the nation.

---

16. See Neuhaus, *The Naked Public Square*, pp. 85, 264.

The particular manner of the churches' presence in the national debates is a sub-issue, one that contains any number of contentious questions. Should the churches endorse candidates? Should they urge specific votes on referenda? Should their tax exemptions be forfeit if they do? How can church activites be separated into the specifically "religious" (constitutionally protected) and nonreligious (e.g., commercial)? Into which category do their schools, or some parts of their schools, fall? Can the state interfere with church practices it deems harmful to the public weal? How may such harm be defined? Must the courts, in order to guard against abuse of the special place granted religion, actually define what a church is, or what religious belief really is? In what particular ways can the state show its benevolence toward religion, recognizing the sentiments of its people, within the spirit of the no-establishment clause? The list is truly endless. I have addressed some of the principles behind these questions elsewhere, suggesting that no neat, principled resolution is possible, that we can only find interim answers, and that this messy but necessary course will work if both church and state practice a mutual forbearance toward one another. For the churches, this means principally not trying to use the state for partisan advantage, institutional self-interest.[17]

Meanwhile the principal point stands, that however practiced, the mainline churches must maintain their commitment to an active involvement in public life. It is even possible that this commitment will become a bridge to reunite them to the evangelicals, as many of the latter have themselves turned from their past rejection of political involvement toward vigorous participation. Several important evangelical declarations have established the principle that Christian discipleship requires such activism; and there are even some evangelical organizations—Sojourners, Evangelicals for Social Action—with specific agendas resembling those of the mainline social action leaders. If the evangelicals really are serious about claiming the heritage of nineteenth-century mainline Protestantism, moreover, they will have to adopt its activist role.

But a confluence of interest is more a hope for the future than a present possibility. For the moment disagreement on substance—often sharp and bitter disagreement—is likely to mask any congruence of principle. The mainline tends to have a liberal social agenda, while much of the evangelical grouping is markedly to the right. The two are not likely to make common cause on, for example,

---

17. See *Church, State, and Politics*, pp. 81-91.

women's rights, abortion, or the course of our foreign policy. Furthermore, as I have long argued, the same principles that argue for mainline church presence in the public debate justify equally the presence there of the evangelicals, and the latter have discovered this fact. The mainline no longer has the stage to itself, and the arguments with the religious right can only intensify. It is also possible that mainliners exaggerate the significance of the new evangelical left out of wishful thinking, a desire to find their own predilections confirmed. All in all, it seems we should be extremely cautious in predicting the return of anything resembling the united Christian front of the last century.

After social activism, a second characteristic essential for the mainline churches should be an openness toward other churches, other religions, other nations. This is not a time for a tradition that prizes universal vision and responsible public behavior to indulge in parochialism. We must not forget, even as we affirm the authenticity of particular religious viewpoints, that we need to look outward from our own churches to our fellow citizens and to the rest of the world. We must speak our word, but with love and charity to those who do not share our religious convictions. Our nineteenth-century forebears, out of cultural blindness, were less than open to what others might possess of value, and evangelicals in our day will be making a mistake if they perpetuate that blindness by encouraging American political messianism, perhaps, or by treating outsiders solely as potential converts to be remade in the evangelical image.

We do well to remember that the "secularist" opposition to vigorous religious participation in the public square is not based on an irrational fear but on real experience. I am not really surprised by the comments of M. J. Akbar, editor of the Calcutta newspaper *The Telegraph*, who argues that Indian experience *confirms* that secularism is the only satisfactory basis for nationhood, that the Pakistani theocracy shows the failure of a religious basis. To "believe that religion is a sufficient basis for nationhood," he writes, goes "against all the evidence of history, not only in this [Asian] subcontinent but in Arabdom and Christendom."[18] It is a sweeping indictment, and it puts us on the defensive. The peril of fanaticism resides in any religiously based politics, because the authority of God is not subject to compromise. Fanatics do not believe themselves accountable to those outside their circle of faith. They make natural totalitarians rather than natural democrats.

---

18. Akbar, *The New York Times*, 3 August 1986, p. E3.

To enter the political arena armed with religious convictions means, in a working democracy, to renounce this fanatic impulse firmly and be willing, truly willing, to make the practical compromises a pluralist society requires without abandoning one's religious convictions. This is perhaps not an art that comes without practice, but it can be done. For now I would say that the mainline churches have, by and large, learned to do it. It was a painful transition, admittedly, as a look at our history will amply demonstrate. But now it is over. Though the evangelicals are well behind the mainliners here, some of their social activists, too, have begun to learn the political limits of righteousness and the practical virtues of coalition and compromise. Even in the painfully difficult matter of evangelism, where openness is put to the acid test (How do we both proclaim the gospel and respect other faiths?), there is evidence that American evangelicals are learning what pluralistic America has forced the mainline to accept. In 1981, to give a striking example, the Southern Baptist Convention formally rejected the idea of defining Christian faith for everyone and seeking to impose it on all Americans, citing both the Constitution and traditional Baptist devotion to the separation of church and state.[19]

Openness to others is not all a matter of compromising one's convictions for practical benefit, of course. There are also positive Christian reasons for this stance, such as acceptance of the other in love, an appreciation of our own imperfect understanding of the Gospel, and awareness of the provisional character of this age. But since such reflections have not sufficiently inhibited would-be theocrats in the past, we church people would do well to walk modestly and assure those who fear us, who seek safety in secularity, that we mean to contribute in good faith to the debates of the pluralist society without trying, openly or covertly, to coerce conversions. I believe mainline leaders today have understood this necessity. They may even be overly modest in setting forth their faith convictions, as many critics believe, but that is better than being intolerant, especially should such intolerance be backed by the power of the state.

The third characteristic on my list of traits and practices the mainline churches must preserve is ecumenism, an active concern for the unity of Christ's church—unity across divisions of history, polity, theological formulation, race, class, gender, whatever has kept Christ's people apart. The classic ecumenical problem is the form this unity should take and how room for diversity is to be

---

19. See Handy, *A Christian America*, p. 208.

found within it. I cannot begin to recapitulate the discussions of this problem that have gone on for years among serious ecumenists, delving into the role of conciliarism, the function of confessional families, the meaning of "all in each place one," the need for mutual recognition of ministry and sacraments, and so on. I argue simply that an honest, open, serious quest for Christian unity, born of a sense of the sinfulness of our divisions and driven by obedience to divine command, must continue to be a major commitment of the mainline denominations. (And would that it be so in the rest of Christendom as well.) These are the churches that helped give birth to the modern ecumenical movement and have been prominent among its champions ever since.

Ecumenism has suffered some setbacks and is perhaps going through a period of relative unpopularity, all too often inflamed by the distortions of its enemies. But the imperative remains. In the face of Roman Catholic ambiguity and evangelical hostility, mainline Protestants need more than ever to preserve the vision. The World and National Councils of Churches need their support—not uncritically I hasten to add, but always with the kind of criticism that is meant to enhance rather than destroy. Those slow, patient efforts to remove ancient barriers, like the World Council's Faith and Order Commission and the American Consultation on Church Union, deserve special support just now, for I believe they have actually brighter prospects for ecumenical gain than common social action.[20] They may yet surprise us with the next great advance and help shape a rich, distinctive Christian voice marked off clearly from secularism and other faiths.

Like activism and openness, ecumenism is an imperative particularly relevant to our world today. Quite aside from the inherent Christian reasons for each of these three courses, the mainline would be foolish to abandon any of them. Indeed it cannot abandon them without ceasing to be the public tradition it has always been in America. Speaking in this large outline, and allowing for all manner of change and improvement within these broad contours, I would say to the mainline still, "Keep the faith."

I have no special wisdom as to what the future will bring, but I can think of at least two developments that may help the mainline to stay its course, or courses. One is the growing possibility of true dialogue with the American evangelicals, who as they enter public

---

20. See my *Barriers to Ecumenism: The Vatican and the World Council of Churches on Social Questions* (Maryknoll, N.Y.: Orbis, 1983).

life themselves will begin to respond to many of the forces that have helped shape the mainline churches. The differences are certainly not going to disappear. The localism of American church life, preserved by the self-selected affinity of strictly voluntary organizations, guarantees that differences will be institutionalized and partly protected from ecumenical reproach. And there is a lot of mutual hostility to overcome, whether the inevitable result of history or the avoidable legacy of fractious personalities. But self-isolation is increasingly difficult in this pluralistic nation, and righteous claims to possess the whole of any truth, even Christian truth, are less credible than ever. From both sides there are encouraging signs that diversity is acceptable. The two may yet reach out to one another. No one who cares about the future of American Christianity should do anything to impede the rapprochement.

The other positive development is the growing impact on American churches of Third World Christianity. It comes to us—comes back to us, often—as something different from our own, not bearing our history and our quarrels, at least not in the same way. It enlarges our view of the church. It invites not neccessarily our imitation or our uncritical approbation but at least our reflection and response to its own new ways of being Christian. Third World Christianity may, as Richard Hutcheson has suggested, contribute to the resolution of our domestic church impasse by showing to the mainline the viability of vigorous evangelical theology and to the evangelicals the Christian necessity of social activism.[21] Its continually growing presence in the World Council of Churches gives fresh vigor to the ecumenical imperative. Its often precarious life as a minority in a hostile religious environment or a suspect presence in a dictatorial state show American Christians new meanings of discipleship, deepening by contrast our understanding of the church's place in our own culture. In these and other ways, it is reasonable to hope, these Christians may contribute new strength to traditional American churches.

I have saved till last, appropriately, the most important thing that can happen to mainline American Protestantism. I would list it as another characteristic to be consciously sought were it within the scope of human achievment, but it is not just another strategy. I am speaking of theological renewal, the timing of which is beyond our contrivance, and in the coming of which one may, perhaps, see the

---

21. See Hutcheson, *Mainline Churches and the Evangelicals*, pp. 89ff., 169-71.

work of the Spirit. It follows, obviously, that we cannot say much about the content of that renewal. Speaking only from the perspective of what might be helpful to the mainline, I would hope that we would see a strong recovery of a sense of the transcendent presence along with a high level of individual commitment and personal faith undergirding the public life of the churches. If I try to say more, I will probably only betray my nostalgia for neo-orthodoxy, though I know well enough that the new never really repeats the old.

The result of such a movement—again, I express my hope, not my certainty—would be a recovery of a distinctively Christian identity, emerging from secular culture not a mere echo of righteous American nationalism and not a dissolved pan-religiousness. It would have confidence and authority without losing its respect and charity toward other views. It would kindle the enthusiasm of the laity once again, supplying a really valid reason for active participation in the life of the Church. And it might, with good luck (needed because renewal movements are frequently divisive), provide a new and powerful centrist Christianity to which many now antagonistic parties might rally.

May such a renewal be in the works? We read that its signs are visible in the temper of our students and in the rise of evangelical movements within our mainline churches, as well as in the much-advertised growth of conservative churches and the cultural "recovery of the sacred." Richard Hutcheson sees a likely sign in the booming, cross-denominational charismatic movement.[22]

I do not have enough confidence in my judgment to read these signs for public consumption. But I do hope—hope in the sometimes latent public virtue of this nation, hope in the enduring Christian faithfulness of mainline Protestantism, hope in a provident God.

---

22. See Hutcheson, *Mainline Churches and the Evangelicals*, pp. 105-8.

Toward a Theologically Informed Renewal of American Protestantism: Propositions for Debate Attested by Classical Arguments

Thomas C. Oden

The premise: Everything required for the future care of American Protestantism has already been providentially offered as consensually received instruction in classical Christian writings. The irony is that these sources are virtually ignored systematically in contemporary preordinal education because of the force of modern chauvinism (the belief in an intrinsic superiority of modern over premodern teaching and hence the inferiority of all premodern teaching) that holds sway as much over Protestantism as the modernity it spawned. Yet theology today must be done amid the collapse of modernity.

I will proceed by offering a series of risk-laden experimental propositions pertaining to the contemporary church and follow each with statements from centrist classical sources—patristic to Reformation, all before 1700. These propositions constitute a potential but not yet actual agenda for the renewing church. This procedure suggests that the renewal of the church does not depend on compulsive attentiveness to the methods, analyses, or ideologies of modernity. Luther had ninety-five theses, Kierkegaard only one; I shall try a middle course with forty-seven.

In presenting the texts I do, I am not pretending any sort of completeness but simply making a preliminary suggestion of typical resources in the classic Christian tradition for reconceiving certain recalcitrant contemporary dilemmas. No single text fully develops its thesis (each is suggestive of other sources rather than definitive in itself). I have arranged them in a particular (though perhaps not self-evident) order in hopes of conveying a cohesive line of argument in a preliminary form.

The method of this exercise is as crucial as (or more so than) the content of these texts, for I am using it to try to show that my premise—that everything needed is providentially given already in the classic tradition—is in fact plausible and that these texts (and others like them) are intensely pertinent to our present quandary.

My criteria in selecting the texts included questions such as the following: Do they reasonably give voice to a centrist consensus of classical Christian thinking? Are they understandable without detailed reference to their immediate historical era? Do they have self-evident historical applicability to periods other than their own? Do they connect with our dilemmas today? Are they sufficiently accountable to Scripture?

It is better to stand aside and let the texts speak for themselves than to assume that they must be channeled through an elaborate modern filter of interpretation in order to be made meaningful to us. Doubtless each modern reader will bring a *Vorverständnis* to the text, but I believe these texts have the capacity to penetrate and transmute our preunderstandings.

Admittedly, the direction I have taken here is only one of many initiatives required, and I do not pretend that it is the only way. Nor do I assume that modern consensus about the meaning and import of ancient texts is easily gained. But such study could become a significant part of getting our bearings theologically within the current church and cultural crisis. Study of ancient Christian writers is hardly enough anyway; there must also be an openness to the possibility of obeying what one reads. Obedience to the ancient ecumenical consensus is more important than mere study of it in the quest for theological renewal in a period in which modern Protestant theology is deeply confused, trapped in incipient narcissisms, pantheisms, atheisms, naturalisms, modern messianisms, and failed (but still constantly touted) social and political strategems.

You will enable me to make a more pointed statement, and, it is hoped, to elicit a more useful discussion, if you allow me the liberty to state somewhat roughly and embryonically these propositions in their flat and candid form, blurting them out as it were without dying the death of a thousand qualifications. I know how vulnerable some of them are and regard them as highly imperfect, subject to trenchant criticism, and requiring further debate. This is our purpose, and I welcome your thoroughgoing criticism. I do not present them as if finished, for that might signal that I had unalterably made up my own mind about them. I regard them rather as experimental comic-pathetic theses to be tested in debate.

1. *The renewal of American Protestantism hinges significantly upon the renewal of sacred ministry (ordained, public, representative ministry). Renewal of ministry hinges significantly upon the right functioning of the offices of* episkopos *and* presbuteros. Classical exegetes often spoke of the direct link between disorder in the church and disorder in the ministry:

> Tell me, where do you think all the disorders in the churches originate? I think their only origin is in the careless and random way in which the prelates are chosen and appointed. (John Chrysostom, *On the Priesthood*, 3.10)

2. *Ill-prepared ordinands jeopardize the health of the Christian community:*

> If anyone gives to a man who wants to ruin the church the power to do so, he will himself be to blame for the outrages of his nominee. . . . Why is it that when a decision has to do with war or commerce or farming or other worldly business, a farmer would never agree to sail, nor a soldier to plough, nor a skipper to lead an army, even if he were threatened with all kinds of death? Obviously because each one of them foresees the danger of inexperience. (John Chrysostom, *On the Priesthood*, 4.2)

When ministry becomes fixated on psychological and political ideas, procedures, and strategies more than Word and sacrament, the lack and hunger is felt in the whole body. *Quis custodiet ipsos custodes?* Ordinal examiners. And who watches these watchers? *Episkopoi.* Who watches these? *Laos*, suffering when they fail.

3. *It is no small thing for an ordained pastor to abandon the apostolic tradition:*

> A small thing is not small when it leads to something great; and it is no small matter to forsake the ancient tradition of the Church which was upheld by all those who were called before us, whose conduct we should observe, and whose faith we should imitate. (John of Damascus, *On the Divine Images*, First Apology, sec. 2, Nicene and Post-Nicene Fathers, 2.9:14)

4. *Though the apostolic tradition is to be renewed in each cultural situation, it is not to be amended:*

> Keep the traditions you have received, without making any ad-

ditions or deductions of your own. (Epistle of Barnabas, 19, Early Christian Writers, p. 218)

Admittedly there are unsound traditions that need criticism and revision. The basis of assessing the worthiness of competing traditions is the apostolic tradition, canonically defined by ancient historic consensus.

5. *Recovery of theological bearings will not occur without a determined struggle against* haeresis *(nonapostolic alternatives).* We are no more exempt than other periods. Those who have invented novel or different views *(haeresis)* inadmissible within the assumptions of apostolic teaching must be charitably resisted. Least needed in a period devastated by theological faddism is the spirit of individualistic originality (creativity, novelty, imagination—the virtues of individual self-actualization):

> Those who followed Marcion, were called Christians no more, but henceforth Marcionites. Similarly Valentinus also, Basilides, Manichaeus, and Simon Magus, have imparted their own name to their followers, and therefore are known as Valentinians, Basilidians, Manichees, or as Simonians. Cataphrygians derive from Phrygia, and from Novatus Novatians. So too Meletius, when ejected by Peter the Bishop and Martyr, called his party, no longer Christians, but Meletians. So too when when Alexander of blessed memory had cast out Arius, those who remained with Alexander, remained Christians; but those who left with Arius were subsequently called Arians. Mark well also that those who after Alexander's death communicate with his successor Athanasius, and those with whom Athanasius communicates, are instances of the same rule. None bear his name, nor is he named from them, but all similarly are called Christians. For though we have a succession of teachers and become their disciples, yet, because we are taught by them the things of Christ, we both are, and are called, Christians all the same. But those who follow the other than apostolic teachings, though they have innumerable successors in their heresy, yet for certain bear the name of him who devised it. Thus, though Arius be dead, and many of his party have succeeded him, yet those who think with him, as being known from Arius, are called Arians. (Athanasius, *Discourses against the Arians, 3, Library of Fathers of the Holy Catholic Church, 8:181-82)*

6. *Since apostolic teaching is canonically provided, substandard teaching (with substandard consequences) is self-chosen. Any effort to improve upon apostolic teaching will be substandard.* That is what *haeresis* is, in its root meaning—self-chosen teaching in defiance of the delivered

apostolic tradition. Orthodoxy is distinguished from its alternatives
in that it seeks more to convey than improve upon primitive Christianity.

> Indeed, in almost every epistle, when enjoining on us the duty
> of avoiding false teachings, Paul sharply condemns unapostolic
> views. The practical effects of false teachings are false choices.
> They are called in Greek heresies, a word used in the special
> sense of that deliberate choice that someone makes when one
> either teaches them to others or takes up with them for himself.
> It is for this reason that he calls such persons self-condemned,
> because each has chosen for himself that for which he is
> judged. . . . In the Lord's apostles we possess our authority; for
> even they did not of themselves choose to introduce anything,
> but faithfully delivered to the nations the doctrine which they
> had received from Christ. (Tertullian, *On Prescription against
> Heretics*, 6, Ante-Nicene Fathers 3:245)*

7. *Christianity is a universal human community embracing all languages and cultures, in which cultural diversity is essential to its universality.* The renewing church reaches out to embrace every class,
every culture, every historical and social situation, while seeking to
maintain union with Christ. The world being the object of God's
love (John 3:16), the care of souls encompasses not only the church,
but also the world, the saeculum, the whole secular sphere. The
heavenly city characterized by the selfless love of God and the
earthly city characterized by the godless love of self interact in history, wheat and tares being mixed together in the visible church.

> This heavenly city, then, while it sojourns on earth, calls citizens
> out of all nations, and gathers together a society of pilgrims of
> all languages, not scrupling about diversities in the manners,
> laws, and institutions whereby earthly peace is secured and
> maintained, but recognising that, however various these are,
> they all tend to one and the same end of earthly peace. It there-
> fore is so far from rescinding and abolishing these diversities,
> that it even preserves and adapts them, so long only as no hin-
> drance to the worship of the one supreme and true God is thus
> introduced. (Augustine, *The City of God*, 19.17)

8. *In the modern American environment, where doctrinal pluralism has
been regarded as a virtue and toleration the chief of virtues, there is good*

---

*In this and subsequent passages marked with an asterisk, I have
amended or retranslated archaisms in the text.

reason to listen carefully to the warnings of the early church—not about cultural pluralism but about doctrinal pluralism. The essential cultural pluralism of ecumenical Christianity was early and repeatedly affirmed. Many cultures, languages, and classes were embraced and transformed, but amid this variety there was a rigorous commitment to the unity of the body of Christ under apostolic teaching, to unity in liturgy and sacrament, and a strong resistance to doctrinal pluralism:

> Where diversity of doctrine is found, there must be some corruption either of the Scriptures or expositions thereof. (Tertullian, *On Prescription against Heretics,* 37, Ante-Nicene Fathers, 3:261)*

9. *With the increased Protestantization of post–Vatican II Roman Catholicism, Protestants now are ironically being called to become intentionally more Catholic, especially in the sense that term was used in the early tradition.* It is precisely because the body of Christ has come alive in such varied cultural situations, speaking many languages and addressing diverse historical challenges with flexible means, that all the more energy has been and must again be given to ensure its fundamental unity, its direct continuity with the ministry of Jesus, its visible, organic cohesion in the apostolic tradition, the teaching office, historic succession of faithful *episkopoi,* and revealed Scripture. This requires a continuing battle with self-determined *haeresis,* views different from the apostolic witness. It also requires a steady commitment to nurture in each new historical situation a living sense of participation in the one body of Christ. There is profound pastoral meaning in the early church's search for catechetical coherence, catholicity, and unity in Christ.

> The Church, then, is called Catholic because it is spread through the whole world, from one end of the earth to the other, and because it never stops teaching in all its fulness every doctrine that men ought to be brought to know: and that regarding things visible and invisible, in heaven and on earth. It is called Catholic also because it brings into religious obedience every sort of men, rulers and ruled, learned and simple, and because it is a universal treatment and cure for every kind of sin whether perpetrated by soul or body, and possesses within it every form of virtue that is named, whether it expresses itself in deeds or words or in spiritual graces of every description. (Cyril of Jerusalem, *The Catechetical Lectures,* 18, Library of Christian Classics 4:186)

10. *The early church was just as adamant against schism as against heresy, because schism displayed lack of care toward the church through its divisiveness. The hyper-reformist mentality that loves more its own purity than the unity of the body of Christ may be well-intentioned, but its efforts at reform are often costly, self-righteous, and schismatic.*

> He shall also judge those who give rise to schisms, who are destitute of the love of God, and who look to their own special advantage rather than to the unity of the Church; and who for trifling reasons, or any kind of reason which occurs to them, cut in pieces and divide the great and glorious body of Christ, and so far as in them lies, [positively] destroy it,—men who prate of peace while they give rise to war, and do in truth strain out a gnat, but swallow a camel. For no reformation of so great importance can be effected by them, as will compensate for the mischief arising from their schism. (Irenaeus, *Against Heresies*, 4.33.7, Ante-Nicene Fathers, 1:508)

11. *The church's ministers have not only a right but a solemn responsibility to claim and guard from disruptive teachers those committed to their care.* Gross distortions of Christian teaching (blatant atheism, reductive naturalism, absolutized moral relativisms, etc.) must be intelligently resisted, and those who promote them must be confronted with their apostasies and follies, especially those who hold office as ordained ministers. The civil right to free speech must be defended but not confused with the ecclesial right to exercise guardianship over the tradition.

> For as they are heretics, they cannot be true Christians, because it is not from Christ that they get that which they pursue of their own mere choice, and from the pursuit incur and admit the name of heretics. Thus, not being Christians, they have acquired no right to the Christian Scriptures; and it may be very fairly said to them, "Who are you? When and whence did you come? As you are none of mine, what have you to do with that which is mine? Indeed, Marcion, by what right do you hew my wood? By whose permission, Valentinus, are you diverting the streams of my fountain? By what power, Apelles, are you removing my landmarks? This is my property. Why are you, the rest, sowing and feeding here at your own pleasure? This (I say) is my property." (Tertullian, *On Prescription against Heretics*, 37, Ante-Nicene Fathers, 3:261)

It is tragically worth remembering that Tertullian, who spoke so eloquently out of a deep commitment to Scripture and Christian tradition, himself fell into a rigorist *haeresis*—a warning to all who pass this way.

12. *Those who have once followed a false faith may learn through it how better to proclaim true faith,* according to the Council of Chalcedon:

> For then indeed is the true faith defended with the best results, when a false opinion is condemned even by those who have followed it. (Chalcedon, A.D. 451, *The Tome of St. Leo, The Seven Ecumenical Councils,* Nicene and Post-Nicene Fathers, 2d ser., 14:258)

Hence those of us who have, like Paul and Augustine, spent many years of our lives fighting against the apostolic tradition are now by grace ironically placed in a better position to defend the faith against these very adversaries—our former selves. This providentially enabled experience is not for nothing.

13. *Since ordinal examination must be rigorously accountable to the apostolic witness, and since modern Protestant theological schools lack interest in such rigor, judicatories cannot rely exclusively upon seminaries to form and accredit ordinands biblically, historically, and theologically.* Orthodox, Catholic, and Protestant traditions have all given considerable attention to examination for ordination preparatory to due authorization to care for souls. Although these examinations have differed in content and approach, in all these traditions it has been considered important that candidates be meaningfully and rigorously examined—not merely to ensure that they are academically prepared but also that they are religiously and morally prepared for ministry. Here is a centrist Protestant view, as expressed by Calvin, of the ordinal examination:

> The examination contains two parts, of which the first concerns doctrine—to ascertain whether the candidate for ordination has a good and holy knowledge of Scripture; and also whether he be a fit and proper person to communicate it edifyingly to the people.
>
> Further to avoid all danger of the candidate holding some false opinion, it will be good that he profess his acceptance and maintenance of the doctrine approved by the Church.
>
> To know whether he is fit to instruct, it would be necessary to proceed by interrogation and by hearing him discuss in private the doctrine of the Lord.
>
> The second part concerns life, to ascertain whether he is of good habits and conducts himself always without reproach. The rule of procedure in this matter which it is needful to follow is very well indicated by Paul. (Calvin, *Draft Ecclesiastical Ordinances,* Library of Christian Classics, 22:59)

14. *Careful, sensitive, and compassionate inquiry into the life commit-ments, behavioral patterns, and beliefs of the ordinand is pertinent to the ordination process. There can be no appeals to absolute privacy if the be-havior and integrity of the pastor are central to the assessment of com-petency and suitability for the pastoral calling:*

> Let examination also be made whether he be unblameable as to the concerns of this life; for it is written: "Search diligently for all the faults of him who is to be ordained for the priesthood." (*Constitutions of the Holy Apostles*, 2.1.2, Ante-Nicene Fathers, 7:397; see Lev. 21:16-23)

15. *Ordination is conditional upon due calling, right instruction, and appropriate examination.* Protestant writers have not hesitated to look to patristic councils for authoritative guidance on ordinal examina-tion. The Lutheran systematician Martin Chemnitz urged that ordi-nands be examined on the basis of patterns established in the an-cient councils:

> First carefully test and examine them as to whether they are legitimately called, whether they rightly hold the fundamentals of salutary doctrine and reject fanatic opinions, whether they are endowed with the gifts necessary to teach others sound doc-trine and whether they can prove their lives to be honorable, so that they can be examples to the flock; for this concern we have the very solemn precept of Paul. 1 Ti 5:22; 2 Ti 2:2. The older councils therefore decreed many things regarding examination of those who are to be ordained; these things are found in Gratian, Distinct. 23, 24, and 81. And canon 4 of the 4th council of Carthage, at which Augustine was present, decreed thus: Let one who is to be ordained be ordained when he has, in an ex-amination, been found to be rightly instructed. And the canon of Nicaea, Distinct. 81, says: If any are promoted (to be) presby-ters without examination, church order does not recognize them, because they are ordained contrary to the rule. (Chem-nitz, introduction to *Ministry, Word, and Sacrament*, pp. 26-27)

16. *Ordinal seriousness in liberal Protestantism will necessarily elicit tension between church judicatories and seminaries, but it promises to be a creative tension the long delay of which has made it even more urgent and necessary.* No academic institution can ordain. The laying on of hands is an act of the church, a complex liturgical act that combines, embodies, and symbolizes interfacing themes: earnest intercession for divine assistance and spiritual discernment, acknowledgement of divine calling, infilling of the ordinand with enabling grace, ap-pointment, entrustment, consecration, public blessing, commission-

ing, and sending forth to office. There are at least five crucial elements of the act of ordination, according to Chemnitz: public testimony, commitment of ministry, solemn vow, authorization to teach, and the church's intercession. Lacking any of these elements, ordination gives misleading signals:

> First . . . [the] rite of ordination is nothing else than the kind of public testimony by which the call of that person who is ordained is declared before God and in His name to be regular, pious, legitimate, and divine.
>
> Second: By that rite, as by a public designation or declaration, the ministry is committed in the name of God and of the church to him who has been called.
>
> Third: By this very thing also, as by a solemn vow, he who has been called becomes obligated to the church in the sight of God to render the faithfulness in the ministry that the Lord requires in His stewards, regarding which He will also judge them. 1 Co 4:2.
>
> Fourth: The church is reminded that it is to recognize that this pastor has divine authority to teach, and to hear him in the name and place of God.
>
> Fifth, and this is most important: That rite is to be observed for this reason, that the whole church might, by common and earnest prayers, commit to God the ministry of him who is called, that He, by his Holy Spirit, divine grace, and blessing, might be with his ministry. (Chemnitz, *Ministry, Word, and Sacrament*, sec. 29, p. 136)

17. *The theologically informed guidance of old-line liberal Protestantism requires a postcritical mode of Scripture study—a mode for which few seminaries are prepared.* No preordinal study is more urgently required than the hearing of Scripture as divine address. It is no exaggeration to say that the church lives through the Spirit's address in the written Word. Although the obedient hearing of Scripture as Word of God is often viewed as a distinctive Protestant emphasis, it is surprising how widely patristic, medieval, and Reformation pastoral writers have confirmed it. The Word the Bible speaks is not a passing flurry of human ideas subject to the control of the critic but an eternal Word:

> There are books and books. For some are books written by God, and others are those that men write. The books that men write are made of the skins of dead animals or some other corruptible material, and, as these last for only a short time, the books themselves grow old and in their own way are reduced to nothing, leaving no vestige of themselves behind. And all who read

these books will die some day, and there is no one to be found who lives for ever. These, therefore, being made of dead things by mortal beings who are going to die, cannot bestow enduring life on those who read and love them. They are certainly not worthy to be called books of life. . . . If I can find in a book the eternal origin, the deathless being, and the knowledge whereof is life, the writing whereof is indelible, the sight desirable, the teaching easy, the wisdom sweet, the depth unfathomable, a book whereof the words are countless and yet all one Word, this book will be a book of life. (Hugh of St. Victor, *Selected Sacred Writings*, p. 88)

18. *There is a thirst and hunger for Scripture that signals the church coming alive to God the Spirit. Since Scripture offers God's own address ever anew to the heart by the power of the Spirit, it is to be read and reread and ever again reappropriated in ever new ways in ever new cultural situations and symbol systems, including our own.* The postmodern situation requires a postcritical reading of Scripture. This is more like reading a letter from one's beloved than dissecting layers of historical influence. Luther argued with disarming hyperbolic zeal that

Concerning the letters of princes it is stated in a proverb that they should be read three times; but surely the letters of God— for this is what Gregory calls Scripture—should be read seven times three, yes, seventy times seven or, to say even more, countless times. For they are divine wisdom, which cannot be grasped immediately at the first glance. (Luther, "Lectures on Genesis Chapters Fifteen to Seventeen, 1536," *LW* 3:114)

You cannot read too much in Scripture; and what you read you cannot read too carefully, and what you read carefully you cannot understand too well, and what you understand well you cannot teach too well, and what you teach well you cannot live too well. (Luther, Introduction to J. Spangenberg's *Postil*, 1542, Weimarer Ausgabe, 53:218; *What Luther Says* [ed. E. Plass], 3:1110)

19. *The Bible's counsel cannot be fully grasped by objective historical inquiry without prayer, spiritual attentiveness, and obedience to the divine address, nurtured by conversation with prophets, saints, and martyrs.* We may do harm to others if we rush into the Bible unprepared, "with pig's feet," as Luther remarked, only grabbing what we want to use immediately, or aesthetically motivated by historical analysis, without listening carefully to the divine address:

Since Holy writ wants to be dealt with in fear and humility and penetrated more by studying *(studio)* with pious prayer than with keenness of intellect, therefore it is impossible for those who rely only on their intellect *(nudo ingenio)* and rush into Scripture with dirty feet, like pigs, as though Scripture were merely a sort of human knowledge, not to harm themselves and others whom they instruct. So utterly do they fail to differentiate; and they move about in Scripture without any reverence. That is why so many dare to be teachers. As soon as they have learned grammar, they profess, without any further study, to know theology and say: Oh, well, the Bible is an easy matter! Particularly those do this whose bellies have been distended by the husks of those swine, the philosophers. (Luther, "Sermon on the Eighth Commandment, 1517," Weimarer Ausgabe, 1:507; *What Luther Says*, 1:78)

20. *It is chiefly God the Spirit who searches us through Scripture, not merely we who do the searching of Scriptures.* What the Christian *episkopos, presbuteros,* and *poimen* seek most in the study of Scripture is not objective, historical knowledge of causal influence but the obedient hearing of the divine address.

It is the sight of you, Lord, that I have sought; and all the while in my meditation the fire of longing, the desire to know you more fully, has increased. When you break for me the bread of sacred Scripture, you have shown yourself to me in that breaking of bread, and the more I see you, the more I long to see you, no more from without, in the rind of the letter, but within, in the letter's hidden meaning. (Guido, *The Ladder of Monks*, 2.6, Cistercian Fathers Series, p. 73)

21. *All forms of knowing—historical, literary, philosophical, political, psychological, sociological—may be brought to good use in teaching the Scriptures, provided the divine address is not taken captive:*

It is an ill Mason that refuseth any stone: and there is no knowledge, but, in a skilful hand, serves either positively as it is, or else to illustrate some other knowledge. He condescends even to the knowledge of tillage, and pasturage, and makes great use of them in teaching, because people, by what they understand, are best led to what they understand not. But the chief and top of his knowledge consists in the book of books, the storehouse, and magazine of life and comfort, the Holy Scriptures. There he sucks, and lives. In the Scriptures he finds four things; Precepts for life, Doctrines for knowledge, Examples for illustration, and Promises for comfort: these he hath digested severally. (George Herbert, *The Country Parson*, chap. 1, Classics of Western Spirituality, p. 55)

22. *Theology is free to utilize, without making an idolatry out of, all of the natural, fragmented human wisdoms. The vast arena of modern human learning may itself enter the service of clarifying the divine address in Scripture.* In his eulogy to Origen, one of the earliest models of Christian teaching and learning, Gregory Thaumaturgus (c. 213–c. 270), bishop of Neocaesarea, spoke of the breadth of Origen's interest in understanding the natural world, and its profound effect upon his own theological education:

> He also took seriously that humble capacity of mind which shows itself in our amazement at the magnitude, wondrousness, magnificent and absolutely wise construction of the world. . . . That, too, he aroused and corrected by other studies in natural science, illustrating and distinguishing the various divisions of created objects, and with admirable clearness reducing them to their pristine elements, taking them all up perspicuously in his discourse, and going over the nature of the whole, and of each several section, and discussing the multiform revolution and mutation of things in the world, until he carried us fully along with him under his clear teaching. By those reasonings which he had partly learned from others, and partly found out for himself, he filled our minds with a rational instead of an irrational wonder at the sacred economy of the universe, and irreproveable constitution of all things. (Gregory Thaumaturgus, "Oration and Panegyric," 7, Ante-Nicene Fathers, 7:30)*

The same Origen wrote to Gregory on the manner and extent of Christian freedom to learn from all quarters. It is in this letter that Origen's memorable adaptation of the metaphor of "spoiling the Egyptians" can be found, an analogy of the legitimate use of philosophy by Christian theology:

> Your natural good parts might make of you a finished Roman lawyer or a Greek philosopher, so to speak, of one of the schools in high reputation. But I am anxious that you should devote all the strength of your natural good parts to Christianity for your end; and in order to this, I wish to ask you to extract from the philosophy of the Greeks what may serve as a course of study or a preparation for Christianity, and from geometry and astronomy what will serve to explain the sacred Scriptures, in order that all that the sons of the philosophers are wont to say about geometry and music, grammar, rhetoric, and astronomy, as fellow helpers to philosophy, we may say about philosophy itself, in relation to Christianity. Perhaps something of this kind is shadowed forth in what is written in Exodus from the mouth

of God, that the children of Israel were commanded to ask from their neighbours, and those who dwelt with them, vessels of silver and gold, and raiment, in order that, by spoiling the Egyptians, they might have material for the preparation of the things which pertained to the service of God. . . . How useful to the children of Israel were the things brought from Egypt, which the Egyptians had not put to a proper use, but which the Hebrews, guided by the wisdom of God, used for God's service? (Origen, *Letter to Gregory*, 1, Ante-Nicene Fathers, 4:393)

23. *The hermeneutic of suspicion (well-known to Athanasius and Luther) must be turned back upon radical critics of Scripture who now imagine they invented it. Social-location explanations of Scripture must be seen in the light of the social location of proponents, often members of a self-interested guild of scholars seeking to perpetuate their own schools.* Highly speculative and value-predisposed challenges to the authenticity of the earliest apostolic witnesses have been too readily accommodated by modern biblical scholars supported by church funds and authorized to guide preordinal biblical studies. Current efforts at renewal are authenticated only insofar as they express and embody Jesus' continuing presence. In the light of contemporary New Testament studies, it may seem that unprecedented clouds of questioning have gathered concerning the historical memory surrounding Jesus that diminish confidence in all statements about him. But these challenges have been vexing Christianity from its earliest times. There has never been a Christian century in which no serious questions have been raised about the adequacy of our available knowledge of Jesus. Some of the earlier questioners doubted that Jesus was ever born at all; some thought that he was not flesh but spirit only; some thought that he was not of God; some questioned the accuracy of the reports about him; some thought the resurrection dubious; some questioned the accuracy of the transmission of the early tradition. All these issues that remain—as historical-critical issues of textual criticism, historical criticism, source criticism, form criticism of the oral tradition, and redaction criticism of the editors of early documents—were rudimentarily explored in the first three centuries of the church's life. Do we have an accurate record of Jesus' proclamation and ministry? Do the New Testament gospels, such as Mark, give us an accurate recollection of Jesus? Papias (c. 60–c. 130), bishop of Hierapolis, and one who is reported by Irenaeus to be "a hearer of John, a companion of Polycarp," answered as follows:

Mark having become the interpreter of Peter, wrote down accurately whatsoever he remembered. It was not, however, in exact order that he related the sayings or deeds of Christ. For he neither heard the Lord nor accompanied Him. But afterwards, as I said, he accompanied Peter, who accommodated his instructions to the necessities [of his hearers], but with no intention of giving a regular narrative of the Lord's sayings. Wherefore Mark made no mistake in thus writing some things as he remembered them. For of one thing he took especial care, not to omit anything he had heard, and not to put anything fictitious into the statements. (Papias, *Fragments*, Ante-Nicene Fathers, 1:154-55)

Why was Papias concerned to point out that Mark took special care not to omit anything he had heard or to exaggerate or falsify any report? Doubtless because the question of the authenticity of Mark's report was already under some question. This demonstrates that the early traditioners were intensely concerned with accuracy of evidence. Otherwise why would Papias go so far as to provide his reader in this passage with a deliberate rationale for why Mark's order in reporting the events of Jesus' ministry does not correspond precisely with other available accounts? This is hardly evidence of carelessness, but rather of Mark's avid interest in accuracy in reporting Peter's witness as it had become adapted through preaching to various audiences.

24. *The written Word is the Spirit's sufficient witness to divine revelation. Where conflicts emerge in its interpretation, they must be adjudicated on the basis of Scripture itself, reasoned under the instruction of ecumenical tradition, with patience and love. The literal sense of Scripture applies unless there is metaphorical intent.* Origen dealt with apparent inconsistencies in Gospel narratives in a way that took into account the diversity of the intention and audience of the various evangelists:

The student, staggered at the consideration of these things, will either renounce the attempt to find all the Gospels true, and not venturing to conclude that all our information about our Lord is untrustworthy, will choose at random one of them to be his guide; or he will accept the four, and will consider that their truth is not to be sought for in the outward and material letter.

We must, however, try to obtain some notion of the intention of the Evangelists in such matters. . . . They use in the same way His sayings, and in some places they tack on to their writing, with language apparently implying things of sense, things made manifest to them in a purely intellectual way. I do not condemn them if they even sometimes dealt freely with things which to the eye of history happened differently. . . . They proposed to speak the truth where it was possible both materially and spiritually, and where this was not possible it was their intention to prefer the spiritual to the material. (Origen, *Commentary on John*, 2-4, Ante-Nicene Fathers, 10:382-383)

25. *Early accounts were more accurate, and more accurately transmitted, than heavily biased, philosophically predisposed, Enlightenment-ideology criticism has thought.* For example, autograph copies of original apostolic writings were preserved as late as 300 A.D. to guarantee the authenticity of the apostolic writer. Bishop Peter of Alexandria (d. 311), a scholar who had served as head of Christianity's most famous catechetical school at Alexandria, clearly believed that such copies had survived the two hundred or more years since they had been written, since they were carefully protected by those to whom these revered writings were entrusted:

> Now it was the preparation, about the third hour, as the accurate books have it, and the autograph copy itself of the Evangelist John, which up to this day has by divine grace been preserved in the most holy church of Ephesus, and is there adored by the faithful. (Peter of Alexandria, *Fragments*, 5, Ante-Nicene Fathers, 6:283)

The faithful were guarding an ancient manuscript believed to be an autograph copy of the Gospel of John. This reference is cited here because there were already by that time alternative readings concerning the crucifixion at the third hour (John 19:13-14; cf. Mark 25:25).

26. *The apostles clearly intended that the original teaching of eyewitnesses to Jesus be accurately passed on intergenerationally as the basis for the continuing renewal of the church.* Mainstream Protestant ministries have chosen to work largely without listening to the experience of ancient ministries, the teachings of which are in fact systematically resisted in theological schools that compulsively track a disintegrating modernity.

> I am not talking of anything novel or strange, or raising any new questions. Although I am an instructor of the Gentiles now, I was a pupil of the Apostles once; and what was delivered to me then, I now minister faithfully to students of the truth. How can anyone, who has been rightly taught and learnt to love the Word, not wish to be told the precise nature of the revelations which that Word so openly made to His disciples? Visibly present among them, the Word made His disclosures to them in the plainest of language; though unrecognized by the unbelieving, He discoursed without reserve to the disciples; and because they were reckoned faithful by Him, they

came to know the mysteries of God. (*Epistle to Diognetus*, 2, Early Christian Writers, p. 182)

27. *Amazingly, even amid the collapse of modernity, we remain recipients of the ancient apostolic tradition through Scripture as sufficient witness to all cultures of God's saving activity.* It was no insignificant point to the African theologian Tertullian, writing about 200 A.D., that the apostolic tradition had survived intact during all those preceding generations to serve the body of Christ in his own time. So it has, by grace, once again been delivered to our generation.

> Come now, you who would indulge a better curiosity, if you would apply it to the business of your salvation, run over the apostolic churches, in which the very thrones of the apostles are still pre-eminent in their places, in which their own authentic writings are read, uttering the voice and representing the face of each of them severally. Achaia is very near you, (in which) you find Corinth. Since you are not far from Macedonia, you have Philippi; (and there too) you have the Thessalonians. Since you are able to cross to Asia, you get Ephesus. Since, moreover, you are close upon Italy, you have Rome, from which there comes even into our own hands the very authority (of apostles themselves). How happy is its church, on which apostles poured forth all their doctrine along with their blood! where Peter endures a passion like his Lord's! where Paul wins his crown in a death like John's! where the Apostle John was first plunged, unhurt, into boiling oil, and thence remitted to his island exile! See what she has learned, what taught, what fellowship has had with even (our) churches in Africa! One Lord God does she acknowledge, the Creator of the universe, and Christ Jesus (born) of the Virgin Mary, the Son of God the Creator; and the Resurrection of the flesh; the law and the prophets she unites in one volume with the writings of evangelists and apostles, from which she drinks in her faith. This she seals with the water (of baptism), arrays with the Holy Ghost, feeds with the Eucharist, cheers with martyrdom, and against such a discipline thus (maintained) she admits no gainsayer. . . . Even the rough wild-olive arises from the germ of the fruitful, rich, and genuine olive; also from the seed of the mellowest and sweetest fig there springs the empty and useless wild-fig. In the same way heresies, too, come from our plant, although not of our kind; (then come) from the grain of truth, but, owing to their falsehood, they have only wild leaves to sow. (Tertullian, *On Prescription against Heretics*, 36, Ante-Nicene Fathers, 3:260-61).

Tertullian was writing only six or seven generations after the death of Jesus, and a century after the death of some apostles. Here we find a picture of cohesive unity of a far-flung Christian witness, resonating with what was believed to be accurately transmitted reports of Jesus' ministry and its significance.

28. *The chief means by which the apostolic traditions were preserved through hazardous times were ordination and apostolic teaching:*

> After the death of the apostles there were Guides and Rulers in the churches. Whatever the apostles had committed to them and they had received from them, they continued to teach to the multitude through the whole time of their lives. They too, again, at their deaths committed and delivered to their disciples after them precisely what they had received from the apostles; also what James had written from Jerusalem, and Simon from the city of Rome, and John from Ephesus, and Mark from Alexandria, and Andrew from Phrygia, and Luke from Macedonia, and Judas Thomas from India: that the epistles of an apostle might be received and read in the churches that were in every place, just as the achievements of their Acts, which Luke wrote, are read; that hereby the apostles might be known, and the prophets, and the Old Testament and the New; that all may recognize that one truth was proclaimed in them all: that one Spirit spoke in them all, from one God whom they had all worshipped and had all preached. Widely different cultures received their teaching. . . . And by ordination to the priesthood which the apostles themselves had received from our Lord, did their Gospel wing its way rapidly into the four quarters of the world. (*The Teaching of the Apostles*, Ante-Nicene Fathers, 8:670-71)*

29. *The foremost task of* episkopoi *is that of guaranteeing to laity that the apostolic witness will be made available to them without distortion or deficit. It is for this purpose that the succession of faithful witnesses to the apostles has been a part of sacred ministry (either for its good order or of its essence, as variously interpreted) from earliest times:*

> We find that throughout all those cities where the Apostles did plant Christianity, so that histories of the times have noted succession of pastors in the seat of one, not of many (there being in every such Church far more pastors), and the first one in every rank of succession we find to have been, if not some Apostle, yet some Apostle's disciple. By Epiphanius the Bishops of Jerusalem are reckoned down from James to Hilarion then Bishop. Of those who claimed that they held the same things which they received from those who had lived with the Apostles themselves, Tertullian spoke in this way: "Let them there-

fore show the beginnings of their Churches, let them recite their Bishops one by one, each in this way succeeding other so that the first Bishop of them hath had for his author and predecessor some Apostle, or at least some Apostolical person who persevered with the Apostles. For in this way Apostolical Churches are able to bring forth the evidence of their estates. This is what the Church of Smyrna did, having Polycarp whom John did consecrate." Catalogues of Bishops in a number of other Churches, Bishops, and succeeding one another from the very Apostles' times, are by Eusebius and Socrates collected. (Hooker, *Laws of Ecclesiastical Polity*, 7.1-6, *Works*, 3:143-51, 151-57; *Anglicanism* [ed. P. E. More and F. L. Cross], pp. 353-54)*

30. *Charged with guardianship of apostolic teaching, the episcopal office is by definition a teaching office. The contemporary church will suffer if the teaching office of bishops fails to reflect the unity, holiness, catholicity, and apostolicity of the body of Christ.* The Quinisext Synod set forth the manner in which episcopal leaders must be teachers (although they are not assumed to be the only teachers), prepared to engage in rigorous disputation and accurate clarification of the apostolic teaching:

It behoves those who preside over the churches, every day but especially on Lord's days, to teach all the clergy and people words of piety and of right religion, gathering out of holy Scripture meditations and determinations of the truth, and not going beyond the limits now fixed, nor varying from the tradition of the God-bearing fathers. And if any controversy in regard to Scripture shall have been raised, let them not interpret it otherwise than as the lights and doctors of the church in their writings have expounded it, and in these let them glory rather than in composing things out of their own heads, lest through their lack of skill they may have departed from what was fitting. (Quinisext Synod, A.D. 692, canon 19, The Seven Ecumenical Councils, Nicene and Post-Nicene Fathers, 2d ser., 14:374)

31. *Women are destined to play a crucial, and perhaps the decisive, role in the third millennium of Christianity.* Divine providence has worked uniquely in our time to elicit the gifts of women for ministry. Seeking guidance from the tradition is not impossible or fruitless even in this arena where it is often expected to be. The recollection of the role of women in salvation history is celebrated in this moving pre-Nicene ordinal prayer:

O Eternal God, the Father of our Lord Jesus Christ, the Creator of man and of woman, who didst replenish with the Spirit Miriam, and Deborah, and Anna, and Huldah; who did not think it unfit that Thy only begotten Son should be born of a woman; who also in the tabernacle of the testimony, and in the temple, didst ordain women to be keepers of Thy holy gates,—do Thou now also look down upon this Thy servant, who is to be ordained to the office of a deaconess, and grant her Thy Holy Spirit, and cleanse her "from all that can defile flesh or spirit" (2 Cor. 7:1), that she may worthily discharge the work which is committed to her to Thy glory, and the praise of Thy Christ, with whom glory and adoration be to Thee and the Holy Spirit for ever. Amen. (*The Constitutions of the Holy Apostles*, 8.3.20, Ante-Nicene Fathers, 7:492, NEB)*

This is a prayer to God to enliven a ministry undertaken by women. The key phrase, also found in the ordinal prayers for the diaconate and presbuterate, is: "Grant thy Holy Spirit." It is the prayer of the whole church for the blessing and empowerment of this ministry. It assumes a long memory of the ways in which God has chosen and ordained women and replenished them by the Spirit. There is ample evidence from Luke 8:1-3, Romans 16:1-16, and Philippians 4:2-3 that women were deeply involved in the ministries of the earliest Christian communities. Paul referred to Euodia and Syntyche as "these women who shared my struggles in the cause of the gospel" (Phil. 4:2). He spoke of Phoebe as "a fellow Christian who holds office in the congregation at Cenchreae" (Rom. 16:1) and specially mentions "Prisca and Aquila, my fellow-workers in Christ Jesus. They risked their necks to save my life, and not I alone but all the gentile congregations are grateful to them. Greet also the congregation at their house" (Rom. 16:3-5).

32. *The church earnestly prays for the right calling, inspiring, and fulfillment of prophetic gifts of women amid our present crisis.* That women are recipients of prophetic gifts is a very old view indeed, as may be seen in this third-century (redacted in the fourth century) recollection of the calling and authorization of women to prophesy:

Now women prophesied also. Of old, Miriam the sister of Moses and Aaron, and after her Deborah, and after these Huldah and Judith—the former under Josiah, the latter under Darius. The mother of the Lord did also prophesy, and her kinswoman Elisabeth, and Anna; and in our time the daughters of Philip: yet were not these elated against their husbands, but preserved their own measures. Wherefore if among you also there be a man or a woman, and such a one obtains any gift, let him be humble, that God may be pleased with him. For says He: "Upon whom will I look, but upon him that is humble and quiet, and trembles at my words?" (Is. 66:2). (*Constitutions of the Holy Apostles*, 8.1, Ante-Nicene Fathers, 7:481)

Accordingly, it was not considered a novel or unusual thing in the early church if women received prophetic inspiration. The Jewish tradition had known numerous prophetic women, and the women in the holy family—Mary, Elisabeth, and Anna—were considered prototypes of prophetic Christian women. Models of prophetic women who have at the same time maintained their domestic covenants and responsibilties can be found in both Old and New Testaments. These models had the character not merely of private inspiration but of publicly declared prophetic witness.

33. *Women are not lacking in courage, as sex-role stereotypes often suggest.* Such courage is needed in the present crisis. In the Lausaic History, Palladius recounts the courage of women during the crises of early Christianity:

> I must also commemorate in this book the courageous women to whom God granted struggles equal to those of men, so that no one could plead as an excuse that women are too weak to practice virtue successfully. . . . Among these was the Roman matron Paula, who was mother of Toxotius, a woman highly distinguished in the spiritual life. . . . I knew Basianillia, too, the wife of Candidianus the general; she practiced virtue zealously and carefully and still is vigorously fighting the good fight. And I knew Photeina, too, a maiden of the highest renown, a daughter of Theoctistus, the priest of Laodicea. And in Antioch I came across a woman also of great reknown who held converse intimately with God, the deaconess Sabiniana, aunt of John, bishop of Constantinople. (Palladius, *The Lausiac History*, 41.1-2, 4, Ancient Christian Writers, 34:117-18).

34. *Women who have the competency to teach must themselves be well-instructed in the apostolic teaching in order to be received by the worshipping community.* A repetition of modern feminist themes will not substitute for the apostolic teaching. In African Christianity of the fourth century it was assumed that duly instructed women might have the calling and competencies to teach:

> Widows and dedicated women (*sanctimoniales*) who are chosen to assist at the baptism of women, should be so well instructed in their office as to be able aptly and properly to teach unskilled and rustic women how to answer at the time of their baptism to the questions put to them, and also how to live godly after they have been baptized. (Fourth Council of Carthage, A.D. 398,

canon 12, The Seven Ecumenical Councils, Nicene and Post-Nicene Fathers, 2d ser., 14:41)

The deposit of faith given in Jesus Christ was thought to be a fully adequate revelation as it was grasped by the apostolic writers, but certain dimensions of that revelation have taken an exceptionally long time to be adequately recognized amid the tragic conflicts of history: the sixteenth-century Reformation, the eighteenth-century toleration movement, the nineteenth-century antislavery movement, and the enhanced freedom of women in the twentieth century. Why did such achievements take so long? Why do they remain so partially actualized? Why were they so slow in coming? These are questions of theodicy and largely remain a mystery of human social sin. We remain slow learners with respect to relationships between women and men. The Christian community is still trying to understand fully what was essentially given in the *depositum* of apostolic testimony.

35. *Heterodox Christianity is perennially corrupted by faddism.* When theology views its own period, worldview, symbol systems, and experience as normative for all past and future forms of Christianity, it becomes egocentrically corrupted, nonhistorically fixated upon faddism, and unable to render its distinct service to the worshipping community. The corrective: enriched historical consciousness. Jean Gerson was astounded at how deeply faddism (= "curiosity" tending toward moral relativism) and intellectual pride (= "singularity") had corrupted Christian theology in his time (1363-1429).

> Curiosity is that corruption by which man, having rejected the more useful things, devotes himself to those things which are less beneficial, things which he cannot attain and which are harmful to him. Of course, when one considers the end to which such an activity leads according to time, place, person, generation, station in life, profession and State, then this judgment of what is more and less beneficial changes in accordance with the different circumstances. Indeed, what is found to be harmful and improper for one is fitting and even commanded for another.
>
> Singularity is that corruption by which man, having rejected the more useful things, devotes himself to foreign and unusual teachings. Here, as with curiosity, it is necessary to take the end of the activity into account before a final value judgment is made.
>
> You see, then, that, although by reason of their different subjects their faces are distinguished by various individual features, curiosity and singularity, as is the custom with sisters, are

alike in many ways. Each is guilty of forsaking the more useful things. And each forsakes these things out of a desire to establish its own pre-eminence. Curiosity does it in order to know what is improper; singularity in order to excel over others. (Jean Gerson, *Against the Curiosity of Scholars*, p. 29)

36. *The Enlightenment bias which begins by systematically ruling out faith's response to revelation cannot become normative for ministry.*

O that all our students in our universities would well consider this! What a poor business is it to themselves, to spend their time in acquiring some little knowledge of the works of God, and of some of those names which the divided tongues of the nations have imposed on them, and not to know God himself. . . . Nothing can be rightly known, if God be not known; nor is any study well managed, nor to any great purpose, if God is not studied. . . . No man that hath not the vitals of theology, is capable of going beyond a fool in philosophy. . . . They read divinity like philosophers, as if it were a thing of no more moment than a lesson of music, or arithematic, and not the doctrine of everlasting life; this is that blasteth so many in the bud, and pestereth the Church with unsanctified teachers! Hence it is, that we have so many worldlings to preach of the invisible felicity, and so many carnal men to declare the mysteries of the Spirit; and I would I might not say, so many infidels to preach Christ, or so many atheists to preach the living God: and when they are taught philosophy before or without religion, what wonder if their philosophy be all or most of their religion! (Baxter, *The Reformed Pastor*, pp. 56-60)

The knowledge of God requisite to ministry is not easily acquired in the university. The irony of the corruption of the church through its ministry is that it occurred through an invention of the church—the university.

37. *Naturalistic reductionism that systematically restricts itself to empirical objects, as do many departments of the modern university, cannot become normative for Christian ordinal preparation.*

Sight is restricted in its scope, and it is therefore quite unable to take in very large things; because it is dim, it does not discern those that are very small; and, because it is slow, when it is directed towards distant objects, even though it spans the intervening space, it is impeded by the very distance itself. For it is not sharp-sighted, it does not penetrate inwards, but roves about only over those things that outwardly appear. Moreover it can neither look back to events past, nor forward to those that are to come. I have said this to show you under what imitations this bodily vision labours, since it cannot see a thing that is not planted straight in front of it. And even then, very large objects are beyond it because of their size, the very small elude it by their minuteness, the far-off ones escape it by their distance, and the inward ones are hidden from it by their obscurity. (Hugh of St. Victor, *Selected Sacred Writings*, p. 158)

38. *When theology lusts after and binges with the* Zeitgeist, *it is the church that gets the hangover.* Theology that is inordinately dependent upon undisciplined forms of philosophy, psychology, and political analysis cannot bind Christian conscience and proclamation. Christian counsel, teaching, and praxis must guard against excessive dependency upon reductionistic philosophies, unsubstantiated psychological opinions, and faddist modes of social analysis, a dependency that plagues contemporary preordinal studies. Christian writers recognized early the hidden dangers of a too easy accommodation of Christianity to changing philosophical schools and pretentious worldviews.

> Unhappy Aristotle! who invented for these men dialectics, the art of building up and pulling down; an art so evasive in its propositions, so farfetched in its conjectures, so harsh, in its arguments, so productive of contentions—embarrassing even to itself, retracting everything, and really treating of nothing! From whence do these "interminable myths and genealogies" (1 Tim. 1:4) spring, and "foolish speculations" that are "unprofitable and pointless" (Tit. 3:9) and teaching that "will spread like gangrene" (2 Tim 2:17). From all these, when the apostle would restrain us, he expressly names philosophy as that which he would have us be on our guard against. Writing to the Colossians, he says, "Be on your guard; do not let your minds be captured by hollow and delusive speculations, based on traditions of man-made teaching and centered on the elemental spirits of the universe and not on Christ" (Col. 2:8). He had been at Athens, and had in his interviews with its philosophers become acquainted with that human wisdom which pretends to know the truth while it only corrupts it, and is itself divided into its own manifold heresies, by the variety of its mutually repugnant sects. What indeed has Athens to do with Jerusalem? What concord is there between the Academy and the Church? (Tertullian, *On Prescription against Heretics,* 7, Ante-Nicene Fathers, 3:246, NEB)*

Similarly, Luther wrote,

> In this regard my advice would be that Aristotle's Physics, Metaphysics, On the Soul, Ethics, which have hitherto been

thought his best books, should be altogether discarded, together with all the rest of his books which boast of treating the things of nature, although nothing can be learned from them either of the things of nature or the things of the Spirit. Moreover no one has so far understood his meaning, and many souls have been burdened with profitless labor and study, at the cost of much precious time. I venture to say that any potter has more knowledge of nature than is written in these books. It grieves me to the heart that this damned, conceited, rascally heathen has with his false words deluded and made fools of so many of the best Christians. God has sent him as a plague upon us for our sins. . . . My friends the theologians have spared themselves pains and labor; they leave the Bible in peace and read the Sentences. I should think that the Sentences ought to be the first study of young students in theology and the Bible ought to be the study for the doctors. But now it is turned around; the Bible comes first, and is put aside when the bachelor's degree is reached, and the Sentences come last. . . . What, then, are we to do? I know of no other way than humbly to pray God to give us Doctors of Theology. Pope, emperor and universities may make Doctors of Arts, of Medicine, of Laws, of the Sentences; but be assured that no one will make a Doctor of Holy Scripture, save only the Holy Ghost from heaven, as Christ says in John 6:45, "They must all be taught of God Himself." Now the Holy Ghost does not concern Himself about red or brown birettas or other decorations, nor does He ask whether one is old or young, layman or priest, monk or secular, virgin or married; nay He spake of old by an ass, against the prophet who rode upon it. (Luther, "An Open Letter to the Christian Nobility," 25, *Works of Martin Luther* [Philadelphia Edition], 2:146-51)

39. *It is neither realistic nor Protestant to assume that Protestantism must completely transform or perfect the political order. It is more Protestant to continue faithfully in one's office even when things tend to go very badly, because if one has been duly called and appointed, God's purpose will become manifest in due time, and God's Word will not return void.* Intensified anxiety over the future of institutional Christianity does not contribute to its renewal.

He who will not be satisfied with his ministry until he has converted and Christianized all will never find peace. Abraham found contempt of God everywhere; yet he did not become broken in spirit, but he and his family continued in the true religion and instructed others. So you should not lose courage either but should continue in the office assigned to you by God.

Let Him worry about the success of the Word. (Luther, "Sermon on Isaiah 51," Weimarer Ausgabe, 25:316; *What Luther Says*, 2:952)

40. *Where one meets no opposition, the task has been defaulted. The Word faithfully declared awakens offense and opposition:*

If ministers of the Word desire to be accounted faithful and prudent on the Day of Christ, they must be very sure that St. Paul did not speak empty words or prophesy in vain when he said: "There must be heresies among you that they which are approved may be made manifest among you" (1 Cor. 11:19). Let the minister of Christ know, I say, that as long as he preaches Christ purely, there will be no lack of perverse folk, even among our own people, who will disturb the church. (Luther, *Lectures on Galatians*, Weimarer Ausgabe, 40:37; *What Luther Says*, 2:931)

41. *Reformist fantasies about the human capacity for vast and immediate change are self-defeating. Perfectionistic expectations of a wheat field without weeds or a visible church unblemished are bound to be disappointed, for they do not take into account the fact that the "heart is deceitful above all things, and desperately wicked" (Jer. 17:9):*

Usually ministers, especially when they are brand-new and have recently entered their office, imagine that when they speak, they should gain their purpose promptly and that everything should happen and change quickly. But this is far from being the case. The prophets and Christ Himself failed to achieve this. Things go as men proverbially say: You are too young to make old rogues pious. (Luther, "Exposition on Habakkuk 1:3," Weimarer Ausgabe, 19:357; *What Luther Says*, 2:927)

He who would have, and is in search of, a church in which no dissension and no difference exist among preachers, no insincerity against the First Table, and no outrage and wickedness against the Second Table, will never find his church. (Luther, "Sermons on Psalm 72, 1540," Weimarer Ausgabe, 49:41; *What Luther Says*, 1:288)

Although the visible church is inevitably blemished by faulty doctrines and by the faulty way the faithful try to live out sound doctrine, yet we dare to believe that the church of the living God is called to be, can be, and in some places may indeed be "the pillar and foundation of the truth" (1 Tim. 3:15).

42. *Duly ordained ministers committed to the ministry of Word and*

sacrament are not well-advised to seek political office or exercise partisan political clout. Luther, whose church had suffered through an overextension of the ecclesia into the sphere of political coercion, stated the point in a way that remains fitting for our time:

> To be able clearly to distinguish between these two kingdoms is a great art, for few people make the proper distinction. This is what commonly happens: the temporal lords want to rule the church, and, conversely, the theologians *(die Geistlichen)* want to play the lord in the town hall. Under the papacy mixing the two was considered ruling well, and it is still so considered. But in reality this is ruling very badly. When bishops were still pious, they observed the distinction well, took care of the churches, and let the emperor do his ruling. But their descendants subsequently mixed the two, grabbed for the sword, and turned into worldly lords. The same thing is happening today: noblemen and young lords want to rule consciences and issue commands in the church. And someday, when the theologians get back on their feet, they will again take the sword from the temporal authorities, as happened under the papacy. (Luther, *Christmas Day Sermon on Luke 2*, Weimarer Ausgabe, 34.2:502; *What Luther Says*, 1:294-95)

> A minister must not go in for politics. Christ was the sole Lord, and yet He said to Pilate: You are My lord (cf. John 19:10f.). (Luther, Weimarer Ausgabe, Table Talk 1, #181; *What Luther Says*, 2:937)

43. *Ministry and statecraft are distinguishable caring functions, alike in their office of governance but radically different in their sphere of operation:*

> I admonish you who are someday to become the instructors of consciences and of Christian churches to see to it that you continue to observe the difference [between church and state]. For nothing good comes of a mixing of these two. And this mixing takes place as soon as the prince says: Listen, you preacher, I want you to teach in this and that way on my behalf; do not criticize and rebuke in the way you are doing. Conversely, it is also wrong for a preacher to propose: Listen, you government officials or judges, you are to pass judgment according to my will. (Luther, *Exposition of John 2*, 1538, Weimarer Ausgabe, 46:184-85; *What Luther Says*, 2:937)

In extraordinary matters, but not normally, the church may enter the sphere of partisan political influence. The Westminster Confession stated a Reformed consensus in urging caution:

Synods and councils are to handle or conclude nothing but that which is ecclesiastical: and are not to intermeddle with civil affairs which concern the commonwealth, unless by way of humble petition in cases extraordinary; or by way of advice for satisfaction of conscience, if they be thereunto required by the civil magistrate. (Westminister Confession, 31.5, *Creeds of the Churches* [ed. J. Leith], p. 228)

44. *Christianity gives resistance to the state where it commands idolatry, and prays for the state where it preserves just order. No political authority is absolute, though all political order is providentially given.* Contemporary American Protestantism needs the pedagogy of classic Reformation teaching of the paradoxical relation of Word and sword.

Although governmental authority is an ordinance of God, God has nonetheless reserved for Himself the right to rebuke its faults. And so government, too, is to be censured that the possessions of the lower classes may not be drained by usury and because of bad supervision. But it is not proper for a preacher to want to prescribe regulations to government concerning the price of bread and meat and the manner of imposing taxes. (Luther, Weimarer Ausgabe, *Table Talk*, 5, #5258; *What Luther Says*, 3:1114)

But if it should happen, as it often does, that the temporal power and authorities, as they are called, should urge a subject to do contrary to the Commandments of God, or hinder him from doing them, there obedience ends, and that duty is annulled. Here a man must say as St. Peter says to the rulers of the Jews: "We ought to obey God rather than men" (Acts 5:29). . . . Thus, if a prince desired to go to war, and his cause was manifestly unrighteous, we should not follow nor help him at all; since God has commanded that we shall not kill our neighbor, nor do him injustice. (Luther, *Treatise on Good Works*, 21, *Works of Martin Luther* [Philadelphia edition], 3:271)

45. *The highest governmental officials and power brokers are not exempt from pastoral admonition.* Allan of Lille provided this penetrating instruction on how governmental authorities are rightly counseled by pastors:

O prince, if you wish to judge the earth rightly, judge rightly the earth of your own body. For there is a three-fold earth: the earth which we tread, the earth which we live in, and the earth which we seek. The earth we tread is the material earth, which is to be trampled on; the earth which we live in is the earth of our own body, which must be tended; the earth which we seek is ever-lasting life, which must be cultivated. . . . What will your spirit say to you then, O prince of the earth, when it, a pauper, will judge you on the Day of Judgement, if you have ruled your sphere ill, and unjustly judged the poor? (Alan of Lille, *The Art of Preaching*, 42, Cistercian Fathers Series, 23:154-55)

46. *When confronted by state power, the vocation and identity of the minister of the gospel must be clear. There is no reason to quake with fear in the presence of temporal, governmental power, however massive.*

Batavis is the name of a town situated between the two rivers, Inn and Danube. There blessed Severin had built a monastery for a few monks in his usual manner because he was often asked by the citizens to come to that place, especially in view of the frequent invasions of the Alamanni, whose king, Gibuldus, greatly honored and loved him. At one time the king, wishing ardently to see Severin, even went there to see him. The saint, fearing that the king's coming might be a burden to the city, went outside to meet him. He addressed the king so firmly that the latter began to tremble vehemently in his presence; after they had parted, the king declared to his army that never before, either in battle or in any peril, had he been shaken by such trembling. When he gave the servant of God his choice to demand of him what he wanted, the wise teacher asked him that, in his own interest, he should restrain his people from the devastation of Roman territory, and that he should graciously release those who were being held prisoners by his men. (Eugippius, *The Life of Saint Severin*, 5, Memorandum 19.1-3, Fathers of the Church, 55:77)

47. *Christianity is paradoxically in but not of each emergent cultural situation.* The Epistle of Diognetus viewed the Christian life as existing in a paradoxical relation to the world, holding the world together, yet looking beyond the world.

The difference between Christians and the rest of mankind is not a matter of nationality, or language, or customs. Christians do not live apart in separate cities of their own, speak any special dialect, nor practise any eccentric way of life. The doctrine they profess is not the invention of busy human minds and brains, nor are they, like some, adherents of this or that school of human thought. They pass their lives in whatever township—Greek or foreign—each man's lot has determined; and conform to ordinary local usage in their clothing, diet, and other habits. Nevertheless, the organization of their community does exhibit some features that are remarkable, and even surprising. For instance, though they are residents at home in their own countries, their behaviour there is more like that of transients; they take their full part as citizens, but they also submit to anything and everything as if they were aliens. For them, any foreign country is a motherland, and any motherland is a foreign country. . . . They obey the prescribed laws, but in their own private lives they transcend the laws. . . . They repay calumny with blessings, and abuse with courtesy. For the good they do, they suffer stripes as evildoers; and under the strokes they rejoice like men given new life. . . . To put it briefly, the relation of Christians to the world is that of a soul to the body. As the soul is diffused through every part of the body, so are Christians through all the cities of the world. The soul, too, inhabits the body, while at the same time forming no part of it; and Christians inhabit the world, but they are not part of the world. The soul, invisible herself, is immured within a visible body; so Christians can be recognized in the world, but their Christianity itself remains hidden from the eye. The flesh hates the soul, and wars against her without any provocation, because she is an obstacle to its own self-indulgence; and the world similarly hates the Christians without provocation, because they are opposed to its pleasures. All the same, the soul loves the flesh and all its members, despite their hatred for her; and Christians, too, love those who hate them. The soul, shut up inside the body, nevertheless holds the body together; and though they are confined within the world as in a dungeon, it is Christians who hold the world together. The soul, which is immortal, must dwell in a mortal tabernacle; and Christians, as they sojourn for a while in the midst of corruptibility here, look for incorruptibility in the heavens. Finally, just as to be stinted of food and drink makes the soul's improvement, so when Christians are every day subjected to ill-treatment, they increase the more in numbers. Such is the high post of duty not to shrink from it. (*The Epistle to Diognetus*, 5-6, Early Christian Writers, pp. 176-78)

Conclusion

These are modest, comic-pathetic, experimental hypotheses—comic because they are so out-of-tune with the presumed flow of power, pathetic because so many suffer from neglect, experimental because they are untested and unproven. These texts suggest that everything essentially needed is providentially given already in the apostolic tradition.

The party is over for the "sexual revolution," promiscuity having become a game of Russian roulette in the new era of sexually transmitted diseases. Yet mainstream Protestantism has offered minimal leadership in this crisis. Socialist politics have failed around the world, but Protestant theologians' knees still jerk left. Just as it appears clear that modernity is waning, Protestant theology persists ever harder in trying to accommodate to it. There are two ways ahead for the church—the easy way and the right way. The easy way appears strong and confident but inwardly is weak and dazed; the right way appears weak and stupid but inwardly is strong and increasing in congruence. The easy way (desperate liberalization— our present trajectory) accommodates; the right way (apostolic teaching) resists a culture filled with signs of death.

There is no more fitting way to conclude than with Archbishop William Laud's prayer for the patient amendment of the church, each phrase of which still needs earnest supplication by the present church:

> Gracious Father, I humbly beseech Thee for Thy Holy Catholic Church. Fill it with all truth, in all truth, with all peace. Where it is corrupt, purge it. Where it is in error, direct it. Where it is superstitious, rectify it. Where anything is amiss, reform it. Where it is right, strengthen and confirm it. Where it is in want, furnish it. Where it is divided and rent asunder, make up the breaches of it, O Thou Holy One of Israel. (Laud, Library of Anglo-Catholic Theology, 3:67; *Anglicanism*, p. 638)

The Story of an Encounter

Paul T. Stallsworth

The scene was set. The place was a rather large room on the fourth floor of the Princeton Club of New York. The date was 1 December 1986. The time was mid-morning. More than thirty participants—from universities, seminaries, ecumenical and interreligious institutions, research centers, foundations, and the media—were seated around a conference table decked out in Princeton orange cloths. Their several conversations indicated that some believable futures of American Protestantism, as well as other things, were on their minds.

Pastor Richard John Neuhaus, like a referee before a boxing match, laid down the ground rules for the conference discussion. He also pointed out the general flow of the conference: we would begin with a consideration of historical elements of American Protestantism, move on to a sociological analysis of the current Protestant scene and an attempt to understand the mainline Protestant position, and conclude by "kicking off the New Reformation" (this was said half in jest—but only half) with a proposal for the theological renewal of American Protestantism.

THE PROTESTANT PAST

The Blessing and the Curse of Pluralism

Timothy Smith, who teaches history at Johns Hopkins, opened the historical part of the conference by placing the much-discussed issue of pluralism squarely on the table. "We are accustomed to thinking that Jews and Roman Catholics, along with other immigrant groups in American society, invented pluralism. I do not think that is the case. I think that learning to live in a pluralistically Protestant society was an experience of the Middle Colonies, which laid the basis for pluralism—freedom of religion and freedom from a religious establishment in American history. So Protestant pluralism is the key context into which all the other groups came."

Another historian, George Marsden of Duke Divinity School, agreed with Smith that pluralism had Protestant roots. However, he added, those roots were also sectarian. "Evangelicals contributed to pluralism to the degree that they were sectarian themselves. If you see yourself as a beleaguered sect, then you become a great champion of pluralism, as the Baptists did," said Marsden. Pluralism, according to Marsden, is simply a product of sectarian survivalism.

Yet another historian, James Turner of the University of Michigan, contended for some important distinctions. "There are pluralisms and pluralisms," he began. "First is the denominational and doctrinal pluralism in the early part of the nineteenth century. It has its antecedents earlier than the second Great Awakening and outside the Middle Colonies. There is a common phenomenon of the late seventeenth- and eighteenth-century American colonies: the various attempts to reconstruct state churches on a European model tend to break down for a variety of social reasons. But when they break down, even in places like New England, you have emergent pluralism. You have effective denominationalism by the end of the eighteenth century. And that has nothing to do with evangelicalism—or with the emergence of evangelicalism. The second sort of pluralism, which we identify as appearing in the late nineteenth century, is different in kind. Earlier pluralism is confined within the boundaries of Protestantism—aggressively militant Protestantism. It is strongly anti-Catholic, for example." But the wide canopy of the second kind of pluralism, which was erected in part because of immigration, covered various religious, ethnic, and intellectual groups. The intellectual dimension of this pluralism even permitted not-believing-in-God to become a respectable option, Turner noted.

Then Turner discussed today's pluralism, his third type of pluralism. "The cement that held the whole thing together before the twentieth century disappeared. It disappeared ethnically. It disappeared in terms of denominational commitments. It disappeared in terms of rough intellectual consensus even that a God exists. That kind of breakdown gave us the sort of pluralism that we deal with in twentieth-century America. It is a very, very different kind of pluralism." In fact, Neuhaus added, today's pluralism can almost be called fragmentation.

Having kept silent to this point, the Reverend William Willimon, the minister to Duke University, was now ready to speak up. "Our conversation has revolved around the issue of pluralism—what it is and what its origins are. That is typical of a lot of Protestant discussion. There has been a lot of intellectual energy expended on trying to establish commonality, cement for our society, I suppose partly from our fear that unless we can establish some commonality, if we all take religious particularities too seriously, there is a possibility of the whole thing blowing apart. But we should remember that Professor Smith's paper deals not only with pluralism but also with the experience of moral transformation. That has been central to the American Protestant experience. Professor Smith shows this in his *Revivalism and Social Reform*. What interests me is that the only discussion that many Protestants can have now is about social and political transformation, rather than what Protestants (at least Wesleyans) began talking about—that is, personal moral transformation, or sanctification. For instance, the United Methodist bishops' recent statement on nuclear arms is mostly a statement about national politics. It contains very little talk about how you might transform Methodists into being peaceable people. We have stopped being interested in that project and are more interested in how to transform Congress."

Tom Oden of Drew Theological School at once lauded the pluralism of yesteryear and criticized the pluralism of today. "Pluralism is a gift, and pluralism is a curse. The pluralism of the Middle Colonies represents an enormous achievement in American society." Today we are at a very different place, he suggested, and then joined Willimon in contending that, as far as the Church is concerned, pluralism and its virtues are not enough. "We need to affirm the virtue of tolerance. We all need each other's tolerance enormously. But tolerance can become a kind of indifferentism. Those of us who dwell in mainline Protestantism are really afflicted with this disease of what might be called theological indifferentism or ideological pluralism or inclusiveness. A part of our task is to provide a critique of pluralism, at least from within the dialogue about theology, for we cannot enter into theological dialogue unless we have identity. The reason that a social transformationist metaphor does not work very well in a denomination like the United Methodist Church, for example, is that the personal transformationist themes have not been adequately focused upon. The reason a synthesis metaphor or a golden-mean metaphor does not work very well for us is that we have tended to lose or diffuse our identity too much. The challenge of centering is what faces us today, and we do not get it by synthesis. We do not get it by tolerance. If you are thinking in Hegelian categories, what we need is an antithesis in order to struggle toward a new synthesis. But that antithesis has not been stated."

Neuhaus responded that fundamentalists and evangelicals believe that the antithesis is "secular humanism." Oden said he had another in mind—namely, "orthodoxy."

An Evangelical Consensus

Evangelical Protestantism gave American society not only the gift of pluralism, but also a consensus of belief, historian Smith asserted in his paper and in his conversation. The evangelical consensus was rooted in widely held and culturally formative beliefs about the Bible, personal transformation, and evangelism.

"Ours was a biblical culture in the nineteenth century," said Smith. "That's one of the factors that made it easy for believers in Judaism and possible for Roman Catholics to integrate themselves into the larger Protestant culture. Second, there was the centrality of a personal experience of religious or spiritual or moral transformation, which all sects came to believe in. By the latter part of the nineteenth century in nearly every religious community there was a tremendous aspiration of faith or belief or confidence in a moment of grace in which an individual entered into a newly transformed moral life, was cleansed of his evil, and in one way or another settled on the path of what the Hebrews call righteousness or justice and what Protestants call salvation. And third, there was the idea of mission, evangelism, proselytizing."

These three characteristics define evangelicalism to this day, Smith observed. However, the characteristics today have a somewhat different meaning than they had in the nineteenth century. Contemporary evangelicalism has traded a simple view of the wholeness of Scripture for the complexities of biblical scholarship. Furthermore, today's versions of the "new birth" tend to downplay the moral and social consequences of spiritual transformation. And finally, to too great a degree evangelicalism today leaves the tasks of evangelism and mission up to the preachers on television. The evangelical consensus, Smith was suggesting, has been watered down.

Smith then noted several places where the evangelical consensus can be clearly seen today. First, it can be spotted in conservative churches "that cling to the Bible, to a literally understood Bible, to a verbally inspired and inerrant Bible." Also, it can be discerned among the pastoral leadership of those churches. "In the average workaday Bible Baptist church or Southern Baptist church or conservative Presbyterian church or Nazarene church or Evangelical Wesleyan church, the pastors feel a close kinship." Finally, the evangelical consensus is in evidence, Smith contended, among the readers of *Christianity Today* and in the National Association of Evangelicals.

At this point Nancy Ammerman from Emory University's Chandler School of Theology reminded Smith of the importance of cultural shifts beyond the evangelical world. "We no longer have that kind of biblical consensus in the culture at large, so that the evangelical consensus of the nineteenth century is by definition very different from the evangelical consensus today. Though today's evangelicals may be linked historically with nineteenth-century evangelicals, they are also fundamentally different in that they are living in a different cultural context. It's one thing to be an evangelical when everyone else is an evangelical; it's another to be an evangelical when you are a lone voice crying in the wilderness."

Backing up Ammerman, Princeton's John Wilson proceeded to list some of the cultural changes that have surely impinged upon evangelicalism: expanding government, redirecting government schools, and proliferation of the media. These changes, urged Wilson, fundamentally affected—and perhaps even undermined—the once-dominant evangelical consensus.

The rise of non–Judeo-Christian religion in America was bound to affect the consensus as well, remarked Wade Clark Roof of the University of Massachusetts. "I just finished doing a fairly detailed statistical review of the American religious landscape," he said. "I find more Muslims in the United States today than Episcopalians. And if present growth rates continue, there will be more Muslims than Jews in the United States before we get to the end of this century. What concerns me is that we keep talking about Catholic, Protestant, and Jewish. In some official way that makes sense. But in a pragmatic, sociological sense it is a statistical fiction."

Roof's statement was seconded by Elliott Wright of the National Conference of Christians and Jews. "We Protestants have not noticed that there is somebody else in American society. In fact there are a great many people here that are not Protestant. And it is not only a question of Roman Catholics and Jews but also of Muslims, Hindus, and various other sectarian groups. This raises very significant questions about the nature of our pluralistic society and about Protestant culture. Recently I was trying to draft a very simple little statement on religious liberty for Religious Liberty Day. It was very interesting trying to write something to cover Protestants, Catholics, Jews, Sikhs, Buddhists, and Hindus on the question of religious liberty. None of the presuppositions about the nature of religious liberty that I learned as a Protestant and as a child of the Enlightenment worked when it came to Hindus and Buddhists. We in the West assume that religious liberty is a part of the good creation of God and is given to us along with creation. Hindus and Buddhists don't believe that. And it is meaningless to Muslims. So you fall back on a constitutional guarantee, turning the Constitution into a kind of scripture. Protestantism may not be the standard anymore."

Neuhaus supported Wright. He said that Smith appeared to be arguing that "for a long time in a constitutive sense evangelical meant American, and that Roman Catholics, Lutherans, Jews, and all others have had to accommodate to that reality." But Neuhaus was not sure about that, especially with regard to the present. "Is that an accurate reading of the way America once was? It clearly is not an accurate reading of where the Roman Catholic Church, the American Jewish Committee, or a number of other institutions are now with respect to the evangelical consensus."

Dennis Campbell, the Dean of Duke Divinity School, briefly noted the rise and fall of the evangelical consensus in the life of the private American university. "The major private universities, which at one time were an engine of the evangelical consensus, are no longer that. Those institutions are confused about their identity," Campbell lamented.

Smith agreed with and broadened the Campbell analysis: "Secularization theories are particularly apt when you apply them to that narrow range of human activity which we call the intellectual community. The history of any of the great private urban universities—Denver, Cincinnati, Vanderbilt, and Boston, for example—is a classic case in point. In the middle of the nineteenth century not just private universities but state universities had a religious center of life and feeling and thought."

Peter Berger, who teaches at Boston University—one of the schools that has fallen from evangelical grace—pondered the meaning and the content of today's consensus. "America is still a Protestant civilization. It was a Protestant civilization when it was formed, and it still is in many ways." Then, after the fashion of sociologists, he got down to cases. "It struck me, if I can be terribly contemporaneous, that the whole Iran-Contra controversy seems inconceivable in a non-Protestant country. In fact, it seems inconceivable outside the United States. I happened to be in Japan when this thing began to break, and there was a blank incomprehension among the Japanese as to what this was all about. They assumed that of course a big power has secret agents running around doing illegal things and having Swiss bank accounts and shipping weapons in secret airplanes. This is definitely a Protestant country in terms of some of its basic assumptions.

"Now, what is that Protestantism that has remained as a consensus throughout the society? That's an emprirical question that is not altogether resolved. I am thinking of John Murray Cuddihy's wonderful piece on 'the Protestant smile' in *No Offense*. That little Protestant smile, that have-a-nice-day kind of thing. That is the outward symbol of the inward evangelical-Protestant niceness that permeates the culture, that created the culture, that makes us assume that our government acts basically like the League of Women Voters. That smile used to come out of a religious context that was undoubtedly Protestant. It seems to me that it no longer does. We have a Cheshire-cat effect: the smile is still there, but the cat has disappeared. To put it in less graphic language, we have a culture today, a highly pluralistic culture, with a number of Protestant forms; but I wonder how much Protestant content remains throughout the culture. I suspect what remains is a set of moral assumptions that are indubitably Protestant in origin and maybe in content."

Less than seriously, Smith asked Berger, "Don't Jews smile? Don't Roman Catholics smile?"

Berger thought for a moment and said, "They didn't used to." The smiles around the table turned to laughter. But after the laughter had died down, James Reichley of the Brookings Institution reminded the conferees that not all Protestants are into smiling—for example, some Calvinists who push a stern morality. That solemn group, it appeared, was not well represented at this table.

But seriously, Turner implored, Berger is onto something when he speaks of a moral consensus. Having earlier spoken of different kinds of pluralism, Turner now pointed to different kinds of consensus: "The years of the evangelical united front, the antebellum years, saw the creation of a kind of consensus on largely moral, as opposed to theological or doctrinal, grounds. That was not accidental, precisely because virtue was so important in the conception of this new republic and in its persistence. Because there was no state church, it became important to mute distinctions in favor of a consensus on virtue. So the evangelical united front is composed of a variety of groups. Wesleyans had one view of the relation of grace to moral action; Calvinists had a different view. What they all did was quite deliberately cloak their differences. The consequence was a highly moralized Protestant culture—moralized to such an extent that it began to look like various kinds of non-Protestant or nonreligious moralism by the latter part of the century. By then it became very easy for Jews and Catholics and everyone else to slide into that consensus, because it was no longer a Protestant consensus in any distinctive sense. It became possible even for thoroughly secularized moralisms to fit into this broad American proposition."

Not entirely satisfied with the reduction of the evangelical consensus to a bland moralism, Mark Silk, former editor of the *Boston Review*, commented that "The notion of a pan–Judeo-Christian evangelicalism harkens back to things some people in this room have written about in earlier days, about whether there is a Judeo-Christian tradition. Are there some common things we can all appeal to? Unlike a lot of people, I think there is some intellectual substance to that notion. It tended to be neo-orthodox, and it focused on the prophetic tradition. And, at least in Reinhold Niebuhr's hands, it was very much antiproselytizing." This was a sign of things to come: later in the conference conversation Reinhold Niebuhr and neo-orthodoxy would play a crucial role.

The Consensus and Politics

It was inevitable. Somebody was bound to bring up the controversial relationship between an American consensus and American politics. The somebody was Richard Hutcheson, Presbyterian clergyman, author, and Senior Fellow at the Center on Religion & Society. "Today the three characteristics of evangelicalism—biblicism, personal transformation, and evangelism—could be applied equally to the evangelical left, the evangelical right, fundamentalism, and Pentecostalism. But when we begin to look at the ways these evangelical groups are engaged in the public square, we see a radical divide, even within the ranks of evangelicalism."

George Weigel of the James Madison Foundation, Washington, D.C., underlined some of the differences in political engagements that he perceived between Roman Catholics and evangelicals. Catholics, he explained, are uncomfortable with directly deriving public policy prescriptions from the words of Jesus, as some evangelicals tend to do. Another source of tension, according to Weigel, is the relationship of personal norms and social norms. Catholics do not go for the radical Niebuhrian separation of the two, but neither do they attempt to project the command to love the neighbor onto the politics among nations, as some evangelicals do. Catholics at their best, Weigel asserted, differentiate the personal and the social realms, assigning different forms of integrity and different norms to each. "These same tensions also exist within the evangelical community itself. The evangelical community is currently sorting out these issues. Using too broad a brush of consensus tends to obscure some very important propositions about how these intuitions, impulses, and tensions are acting themselves out."

Weigel suggested that the Calvinists are not necessarily winning. Calvinism sets up a somewhat smooth transition from personal-church-communal sanctification to public-societal sanctification. In other words, its thinking unifies personal, ecclesial, and civil realms. Therefore, Neuhaus explained, Calvinism grudgingly accepts pluralism as a compromise born of failure—the failure of Christians to Christianize the social order. On the other hand, Neuhaus noted, Lutherans and others who divide (though do not radically separate) the personal, ecclesial, and social realms are not so unhappy with pluralism, for they believe that the Christianization of the social order is a fundamentally flawed goal.

Having endured a brief Lutheran sermon, Smith was now ready with his own. After quoting a past dean of Harvard Divinity School to the effect that Protestantism is an ultimate optimism but a provisional pessimism, Smith referred to Jim Wallis of *Sojourners*. "One should not quickly dismiss Jim Wallis's book on conversion. This is his most serious book. It talks about the necessity of a thorough conversion, involving not only private-personal ethics but also social ethics. That is a much more radical statement than many. But it is not too radical for me. Or Ron Sider's talking about peace and poverty. They suit me just fine."

Wait a minute, pleaded Weigel in self-defense. "I was not urging a retreat into a naked public self with no concern for the social sphere." After all, Weigel reminded the group, Roman Catholics were thinking about the relationship of piety to politics 1,500 years ago. "My concern," he continued, "is not *whether* piety and politics relate but *how* they relate and what quality of thought relates them."

Neuhaus then extended his statement on Calvinism by addressing American Protestantism's "theocratic impulse." "There is a theocratic impulse which has its right-wing form in R. J. Rushdoony and the Christian reconstructionists in California. It has a left-wing form in Jim Wallis. Basically, Robert Handy is correct: the theocratic impulse is the mainline story—namely, the Christianization of America. That impulse, in all of its permutations, brings you to the conclusion that pluralism has not been an intentional achievement on the part of Protestantism in America but has been the failure of everybody's theocratic intentions."

Milton Himmelfarb expressed relief that the theocrats had not won in America. Himmelfarb, a former research director of the American Jewish Committee, said that "one hundred years ago

Matthew Arnold described England as church-ridden, sinking under the weight of Puritanism. He wanted to let in a little Hellenic lightness and air, because it was all too depressing." Perhaps Reichley was right after all: some Calvinists don't smile, even when they win.

No Consensus on the Consensus

John Cooper, formerly of Bridgewater College and now at the Ethics and Public Policy Center, mentioned several of the important divides in contemporary American Christianity: social action/evangelism, biblicism/symbolism, sin/human potential. Cooper expressed a hope for the establishment of a consensus among "Christians of the center" that would take into account, if not close, the divides. Basically, such Christians (and others of good will) should think in terms of a golden mean and should affirm the kernel of truth in all contending parties, said Cooper. They should strive to see God's grace at work in the works and events of human culture. "Even someone like Reinhold Niebuhr said that martyrs, prophets, and statesmen may each in his own way contribute to the kingdom of God."

Ed Dobson of the *Fundamentalist Journal* was not interested in centrist Christianity. He began with a confession. "Fundamentalists are not into history. We're into results: how much money we take up in the offering, how many people get converted, how big the buildings are, how long the mailing lists are."

But then Dobson, ironically, proceeded to speak about history at some length.

"At the turn of the century as evangelicals reacted to theological liberalism, there was an evangelical-fundamentalist consensus, a loosely forged coalition that was essentially threatened by theological liberalism. On the intellectual level, fundamentalists reacted to the rise of the American university and the increased secularization of the private colleges, to the influence of the German university, and to an empiricism that almost implied cynicism, especially with regard to supernatural revelation and the miracles of Scripture.

"Fundamentalists, as a loosely formed coalition, withdrew from the culture at large and began doing their own thing from the 1930s until 1980. It was our commitment to Scripture, to the new birth, and to evangelism that provided the guiding force to that movement. We began in the storefronts apart from the culture, separated from the culture, and totally against the culture. Now, fifty years later, some of the larger churches in communities all across the country are fundamentalist in theology. Not all of them would claim the name fundamentalist, but many certainly grew out of those roots.

"It is unfair to characterize all fundamentalists as obscurantist, anachronistic, pew-jumping, sweat-drenched, snake-handling, Appalachian hillbillies. When one gets into fundamentalism, one finds that it is very complex, very divided. But we each did our own thing between 1930 and 1980—with radio, with television, with publishing, with our own fellowships and denominations—as did the evangelicals. So by 1980 you have evangelicals, and young evangelicals, and worldly evangelicals, and neo-evangelicals; and you have fundamentalists, and hyper-fundamentalists, and neo-fundamentalists, and pseudo-fundamentalists.

"But then a perception grew across the spectrum that somewhere out there secular humanism is destroying what we really believe. And whether it's real or only perceived, to the mind of the fundamentalist it's a threat. It's the antithesis. It's something that's encroaching upon us, like theological liberalism. And so we decided to do something about it.

"Since the 1970s, when we entered into the political process, there has again been a general, loose consensus—a fundamentalist ecumenism that has almost transcended theological roots. At times it has intersected with the Jewish community, although uncomfortably on both sides. It has even granted that Catholics are not as bad as we have been saying they were for the last fifty years; after all, they now have a real nice Pope who says a lot of things that we like. All of a sudden within the political process we began forming coalitions with people who are totally outside our theological roots. Initially, we were very enamored of that and really didn't make an effort to formulate a political philosophy or a theological basis out of which to operate in the public forum. As fundamentalists we were separationist and confrontational by nature. So when we entered politics, we entered to confront the system.

"In the past seven years we have affected the culture and we have been affected by it. In our early involvement we did not understand pluralism. To us, pluralism meant getting in and throwing a few secular humanists around and being allowed to do that. But we have grown more sophisticated. We have gotten in there and said something. But now that we have said our piece, where are we?

"We've got a couple of options. We can smile with the charismatics about the potential of taking over the Republican party and electing a charismatic President. But of course the charismatic smile bothers fundamentalists to begin with, because it says that they have something we don't have. Fundamentalists are not into smiling, because we are an angry movement by nature. We are angry with the culture, angry with what's happening. But in getting involved in the political process, we have been somewhat secularized by the process, co-opted by the process. Now we are caught in the tension between reforming society, which is very public, and revival, which is very personal. So I am not sure where fundamentalism is headed.

"Fundamentalists don't care what the mainline does. We never have, we don't now, and we never will. Our feeling is that the mainline may be the sideline, and we're the sideline becoming the mainline. But we are struggling with where we are, especially in the public domain and in political involvement."

At this point Neuhaus claimed that he saw some light. The light involved "what John Courtney Murray called 'the American proposition.' It has met with affirmation and is now meeting with affirmation from quite distinct communities, particularly Jewish, diverse Protestant, and Roman Catholic communities. This does not mean that Marc Tannenbaum and Cardinal Bernardin are subsumed under the evangelical banner but rather that the evangelicals got there first and put their name on it. It is not the continuity of the evangelical hegemony that is the striking phenomenon in American history but rather the continuity of the American proposition." This proposition, as Dobson's account of the fundamentalist past shows, tempers and changes religious communities and individuals.

Smith closed the Monday morning session of the conference by emphasizing the role of "the people" in creating an American experiment in pluralism and in creating a religious consensus. First he spoke about the people and pluralism. "At Harvard, Professor Schlesinger said that a law is the result of a social process, and you are never told the history of the past if you just tell the history of past politics, past legislation. I do not believe the Constitution created the pluralism of which we speak. It recognized its existence. But the human experience was the story line, the human experiment of people of many different sects and cultures who came to settle in this new world. Out of that experience—and their religious experience certainly came to play in the whole situation—there was created the pluralism with which the federal government was born. The Constitution's brief half-sentences about freedom of religion and freedom of religious expression are the result of a long social and indeed spiritual process."

Then Smith talked about consensus one last time, this time in terms of popular religion.

"Popular religions do not die out. They are like species in biology. They come into existence very slowly, but hang around for eons. There is no chance that evangelicalism and fundamentalism in all of their wonderful variety are going to pass away. What is going to keep them alive is not their dogma, which often degenerates to dogma eat dogma anyway. What is going to keep them alive is not even the wonder of their church organizations, though they do make a difference in the cases of Methodists, Mormons, Roman Catholics, and Southern Baptists. What is going to keep them alive is the persistence of popular religion—popular piety, prayer, the religious training of children. This winds up in some organized religious form. But in back of religious preference, in back of dogma, in back of organization is this basic hunger for God.

"People today are basically transcendent-deprived. They just need God. This kind of impulse lies back of the popular history that I try to write, rather than dogmatic or institutional history. There is a deep impulse in the human character that searches for unity, brotherhood, sisterhood, and kindliness to other people, despite all the known wickedness and violence. If the highest and the best of the popular impulses of modern man have their say, we will wind up with a society in which there exists a common place of prayer, faith, and obedience to a God of righteousness and love. The people who really believe, who really nurture children, and who are really concerned with peace and love and righteousness—they are the people who are going to persist in society."

On that note of bold hope, the conference's first session ended.

PROTESTANTISM TODAY

The Kulturkampf in Church and Society

James Hunter of the department of sociology at the University of Virginia led off the afternoon session by surveying the present Protestant scene. In a nutshell, Hunter reported that a Kulturkampf, a culture struggle or culture conflict, is taking place in American culture and therefore in American Protestantism. It pits the old or business or bourgeois class, with its religion of "orthodoxy," against the new knowledge class, with its religion of "progressivism."

Perhaps exhibiting a touch of sociological imperialism, Hunter redefined a couple of key words in the terms of the Kulturkampf. For starters, he defined *pluralism* as "a competition on the part of different moral traditions to define reality." The current competition within Protestantism involves two basic forces, he explained—"orthodoxy, which has a commitment to an external, definable, transcendent truth, and progressivism, which resymbolizes historic faith." Even *ecumenism* was defined, or redefined, as "a form of cooperative mobilization" by forces in the cultural wars of Protestantism.

After looking at the troops, generals, organizations, strategies, and vitalities of the contending forces, Hunter turned to some of the trends in American public life that seem to favor the progressives. In particular, he mentioned the expanding autonomy and power of government, the rapid growth of the secular cultural establishment, and the increasing portion of the population that is exposed to the secularizing influences of higher education and sectarian schooling.

Moderator Neuhaus noticed a contradiction, or what he thought to be a contradiction, in Hunter's presentation. "James Hunter criticizes the social-science establishment for saying that religion is epiphenomenal (i.e., that it is derivative), and yet is not the conceptualization Hunter advances suggesting that the phenomenon is a Kulturkampf, a cultural war of moralities in conflict, of which religion is indeed epiphenomenal in the sense of being an expression of that?"

Berger answered that this is not an either/or question. Instead, he posited, "we are dealing here with an interaction. To say that religious symbols are used in a class conflict does not mean that religion is an epiphenomenon. For example, one can make a plausible argument that the Protestant Reformation involved all kinds of power struggles and class struggles and that it had nothing to do with religion. But that does not mean that Luther was not sincere in his religious crisis."

Smith College's Tom Derr took issue with Hunter on one of his redefinitions. "Hunter's ecumenism becomes a combination for advantage. This doesn't accord with any ecumenism that I know. The missing factor is the engine that really drives ecumenical cooperation, which is the sense of the sinfulness of division. Unfortunately, Professor Hunter's paper describes the religious phenomenon in a way that is disassociated from the self-understanding of the involved actors. So it is not really describing the phenomenon at all."

Neuhaus also expressed uneasiness with the sociological definition of *ecumenism*, but he tolerated it: "Whatever the professional ecumenists understand themselves to be doing, it is collaboration for advantage in the way they define reality, to use the terms of contestation."

At this point Wright traced the origins of several words in the discussion. "*Mainline* is an old railroad term. It is a word of description from geography about the way towns were built on the American frontier. Churches that got there first were on the mainline, and everything else—the Catholic churches and Baptist churches—was on a back street. I'm not sure *mainline* is a helpful term. I think *oldline* is better. *Orthodox* is very much an ecclesiastical term, while the one on the other side, *progressive*, is a generic term from the world of politics."

Then Wright uncovered some messy definitional complexities of the Protestant Kulturkampf. "Orthodox is described as external, defined authority structures; and progressive is described as that which wishes to resymbolize historical faiths. There are some movements, groups, and individuals who would consider themselves within orthodoxy but have in recent times engaged in a resymbolization of historic faith. I think of the PTL Club's American Heritage or Heritage USA, which I visited last summer. The PTL Club is most decidedly a resymbolization of historic faith. On the other side, some of those that you would consider progressive in the liberal camp, even leftist in their theologies, have appealed to an authority structure as immutable as anything I have ever encountered." In fact, Wright stated, some progressive orthodoxies come complete with checklists and inquisitors to seek out those who do not check off all the items on the list.

That Gap

Milton Himmelfarb mentioned that an important manifestation of the culture struggle within Protestantism is the wide gap between the theology and politics of the clergy on the one hand and the laity on the other. A large portion of the Protestant elite is quite alienated from "middle America" and therefore corresponds to the "San Francisco Democrats" who always "blame America first," Himmelfarb claimed. Then he asked, "Why is there no 'revolt of the Protestant masses'?"

Hunter replied that there is, but it is a subtle, bloodless revolt. Laity dissatisfied with denominational leadership often become inactive church members or join another church or leave the church altogether. Usually, Hunter guessed, this is done with very little fanfare.

Reichley also believed the revolt is here, or at least very near. He pointed to the forces within the mainline churches that are demanding programmatic and financial disclosure from their denominational and ecumenical bureaucracies.

The laity indeed are stirring in the mainline, remarked Hutcheson. "Much of the financial support for television ministries comes from mainline people. I think that's generally true of a lot of parachurch ministries. The effect on the mainline churches is like the effect on the Presbyterian Church, which right now does not have enough money to reestablish new headquarters. Also, renewal movements within these denominations are having a very significant effect. My reading, as an outsider, of the last United Methodist General Conference is that the impact of some of these movements on that conference was substantial. It is in other denominations as well. Also, the fact that the center of gravity of church life has moved to the local church is a significant element of what has been happening to mainline churches."

Neuhaus highlighted Hutcheson's list by mentioning the Good News movement within United Methodism and the Presbyterian Lay Committee within Presbyterianism.

Change is indeed in the mainline air, but Dean Kelley, who works at the mainline of the mainline, the National Council of Churches, wanted to be very clear about that change. "There is a resonance within mainline-oldline ecumenical bodies to more traditional concerns, but I don't think it comes from feeling chastised, defensive, or self-protective. It is just like much of the rest of the culture—leaders have begun to hear that sort of concern more plainly. Some things may have made their hearing more acute, but I don't think the mainline interest in traditional concerns should be viewed as just a defensive response.

"But there still is that gap between the leadership and the laity. It does stem in large part from professional higher education. It may be a generation gap. It may be a culture gap between cosmopolitan and localist elements or between higher education and those outside that sphere. There are a lot of components of the gap. But one of the least of them is political.

"You can call it freedom of the pulpit or simply apathy, but I think congregations can put up with a lot of nonsense of a political nature from the pulpit. Their tolerance seems to be immense, perhaps because they don't take the preacher that seriously to begin with, at least when he's talking about politics. They can put up with that if he gets back to religion eventually. I do not endorse that differentiation between religion and politics, but some people do. The fact that the preacher is inveighing against American intervention in El Salvador and drumming up trade for the Sanctuary Movement, both of which I would agree with, is not going to have a great deal of effect upon the members of the congregation. It is not disaffection from the political views of the clergy that contributes to the decline in membership in mainline churches. What is contributing is dissatisfaction—not with the so-called political preaching but with the clergy being seen, and rightly so, as not ministering to the religious needs of the people in the pews. Politics is not in it. It is that the minister is not meeting their most immediately felt religious needs."

It was later suggested that to the degree that politics substitutes for or replaces religion, it is a cause of mainline decline. Many agreed.

Jean Caffey Lyles of *The Lutheran* accepted the existence of a gap between clergy and laity, but she was more interested in the gap between mainline churches and evangelical churches. That gap is closing, she suggested, as both sides move toward the center. "The center of gravity of American Protestantism is moving away from the Northeast to the Midwest, and to some extent to the South. I see this in the fact that Fuller Theological Seminary is becoming more important. Someone mentioned to me that Fuller educates more Presbyterian Church (USA) clergy than Princeton does. There is a growing prestige of schools like Calvin College, Wheaton, Duke, and Emory. Fuller, Calvin, and Wheaton are moving toward the middle, where they become more like the mainline.

"The religion reporters that I hang out with used to say that the job they'd really like to have was the *New York Times*. They don't say that anymore. They say the job they'd really like to have is the *Chicago Tribune*. Also, the merging denominations' headquarters—the Presbyterians and the Lutherans—are both apparently moving to the Midwest. And there are other churches that are talking about this."

Lyles saw similar moderating movements in other places as well. "The evangelical parties or caucuses are succeeding in getting more nuanced pro-choice statements out of mainline denominations. The major Protestant magazines are also publishing more nuanced articles. For instance, *Christianity and Crisis* did a forum on abortion. Everyone in the forum was pro-choice, but even someone like Beverly Harrison, who has written probably the farthest left pro-choice book, acknowledged there were some instances when a woman should not have an abortion. This is an important concession for people that far left on abortion rights." Lots of groups are striving for middle ground in the Lyles analysis, so the Protestant Kulturkampf might turn out to be shorter and/or less intense than some expect.

Silk was not entirely convinced by a new-class analysis of the clergy-laity gap. His source was history. "It is worth keeping in mind the historical dimension of the chasm that we are discussing.

There were abolitionist clergy. There were surveys taken before the First and Second World Wars on pacifism among clergy that show there was radicalism in economics and socialism then too. So there is really a tradition of that kind of thing."

Neuhaus promptly offered a strong second to Silk. "If you look at this historically, the oldline-mainline clergy have been in the past much farther 'left' by ordinary definitions of issues than the National Council of Churches or the United Methodist General Board of Global Ministries would be perceived today. And yet in the 1930s people were not talking about the gap between clergy and laity. What Reinhold Niebuhr railed against—the sentimental liberalism and the soft and hard utopianism of the clergy—was in the 1930s much more pronounced than would be generally the case today."

Dean Curry of Messiah College reported that what Reinhold Niebuhr railed against has crept into the evangelical camp, opening up a chasm and engendering competition. "This is *the* intramural struggle going on within evangelicalism today. There is the orthodox fundamentalist understanding of evangelicalism, which is very exclusivistic in its theology. There the stakes are high. They are ultimate. There the truth is not divisible. According to this understanding, somebody is right and somebody is wrong, and where you come out has eternal kinds of implications. The orthodox fundamentalists are pitted against the progressive evangelicals. This group has been heavily influenced by new-class kinds of ideas. For this group the boundaries of theology are not nearly as impermeable. Progressive evangelicals are much more willing to negotiate the boundaries of their theological beliefs. They also tend to value pluralism in and of itself. Therefore, things like civility and tolerance become important." The leaders of the progressive side, said Curry, are Ron Sider and Jim Wallis. The elite-laity struggle in the mainline, which was well documented in a Roper poll, is certainly not the only struggle in American religion today, Curry seemed to be reminding the group. Still, it is an important one.

Trouble and Promise in the Seminaries

The clergy-laity conflict pertains to "the most pressing and troubling dilemma facing theological education today, and particularly theological education in the mainline," said Dean Campbell. "Professor Hunter's comments on leadership and his analysis of the seminaries are on the whole quite accurate. This needs to be seen as tied up with the secular cultural establishment and the secularizing effects of higher education. On the whole the mainline has chosen theological education in the context of universities or in the context of seminaries that are free-standing but dominated by a philosophical and intellectual tradition which is the same as that of the mainline university seminaries. The question is whether there is some way that we can get hold of this problem. Is it really the case that, by definition, being part of a university makes a theological faculty inevitably part of the secular cultural establishment? The training of future clergy continues to drive a wedge between clergy and laity."

Campbell expressed grave concern about the work of the mainline seminaries—and especially the one at Duke. "A Roman Catholic priest observed that the greatest question facing Roman Catholic seminaries today is whether the priest can go back to where he came from. I worry about that almost every day. Here we have people coming out of West Virginia, or east Tennessee, or any other place, to Duke Divinity School, and I ask myself whether they can go back home to minister effectively."

Campbell finished by encouraging honest self-criticism in theological education. "The cutting edge is schools that are trying to be self-critical. We have had so much defensiveness in theological education. Most theological educators hearing this discussion would jump on the table with a ringing defense of what has been and what is, in hopes that it can be forever that way. The most significant work might be in those schools that are willing to accept that what is being described here has a large amount of truth to it, that we have a real problem, and that we had better look at ourselves and see how we are functioning in the training of clergy."

Ed Dobson also worried out loud about contemporary Protestant seminaries—all of them. "My hunch is that our seminaries, whether conservative or liberal, are answering questions that no one is really asking. My hunch is that, whether conservative or liberal, we are essentially out of touch with the grass roots." Dobson recalled a recent decision at Liberty Baptist Church in Lynchburg, Virginia, to sponsor a study on marriage, divorce, and remarriage. The seminary crowd opposed the study, however, because it was all caught up in wrangling over the meanings of certain Greek words. The academy knew its books, libraries, and "great exegetical questions," Dobson stated, but it did not know the questions or the needs of the people. "Christian ministry should address and engage the needs of society," Dobson challenged.

As John Cooper looked into the future, he saw the seminaries gradually changing for the better. This change, he bet, would occur through generational replacement. As assistant and associate professors move up the ladder, they will diversify the theological ethos at most seminaries, Cooper hoped.

David Novak of the Jewish Theological Seminary of America implied that seminaries really are important because they might teach their students to mediate. (That's *mediate*—not *meditate*.) "Clergy—in Protestantism, Roman Catholicism, and Judaism—really can and ought to, but usually do not, function as a kind of mediating structure. If you have an elite and you have a laity, the elite are primarily professors or officials of large national organizations. The laity are the people sitting in the pews. Where does the parish clergy come into that picture? They are most effective when they function as a mediating structure. But they have not. In my community the rabbinate (and you can generalize from that to the parish clergy) become one of two things: they totally pander to the laity and have done whatever they thought was popular, or they simply and dogmatically repeat what they think is pleasing to the elite. The most effective in the congregational role are those who have attempted to mediate between those two extremes." Now, mediation, Novak warned, is not taking a little of this and a little of that. Nor is it dulling down sharp differences of opinion. Rather, mediation is a distinct "third function" that, by bringing contending forces into conversation, prevents the deadly polarization Hunter describes. Such prevention, all agreed, would be for the good.

Preliminary Protestant Futures

So where is the future of American Protestantism? In popular religion, answered the University of Virginia's Jeffrey Hadden, who connected with Tim Smith's final comment of the morning session. "What is so critical and important in American religion today is that effervescent rebirth of popular religion. To the extent that the oldline churches, the established churches, are not addressing it, new religious forms emerge. The real core of popular pietism is being reborn and rekindled outside the mainstream of American culture." Sounding like one of Paul Hollander's "political pilgrims," Hadden announced, "I have been to Lynchburg and I have been to Virginia Beach, and I think that I have seen the future."

Then Hadden sketched some institutional consequences of current popular piety. "Some years ago when Jerry Falwell created the Moral Majority, he said his organization was pro-life, pro-morality, pro-traditional family, and pro-American. You can be sure that he looked at public opinion polls. If you want to move beyond those four planks, move to ACTV—American Coalition for Traditional Values—with its ten moral planks, and lay those out beside where the general American public is. This is where the center of culture is moving. To the extent that mainline Protestantism gets on the stick, it will find that it is, over the next generation or so, leavened by this popular religion. If it doesn't, it will continue to experience a period of demise."

Neuhaus asked, "But does that future really work?" Without missing a step, Hadden replied, "In one way or another." Neuhaus was unpersuaded.

Nor did Hadden persuade Peter Berger, who reached for a crystal ball, gazed into it, and foretold this future: "I'm not at all sure that the future is in Lynchburg. I think it's more complicated than that. If one looks at the present Kulturkampf and then asks what prognosis one can make, I would tend to think that it is going to be a very nuanced picture. Here I will make some totally irresponsible predictions. There are three main moral-political areas in which the present culture conflict is most manifest—social issues, economics, and foreign policy. I would see in all of those areas various degrees of conflict and compromise, with no one side clearly winning. If the progressivists are going to win anywhere, my hunch is that it is going to be on some of the social issues. It is very hard for me to believe that the hedonistic trend in American sexual mores is going to be decisively reversed, even by AIDS. Once you have birth control, people are going to act differently than when they didn't have birth control. On economic issues the other side is much more likely to win. Despite the Roman Catholic bishops and their pastoral letter on economics, the economic disaster that would be produced by a liberal agenda has become so obvious that it does not have much of a future. I am most uncertain about the third area, foreign policy issues. I do not know how that is going to come out—superpower, hawkish, macho; or soft, pacifistic-oriented, left-wing Democratic party."

Whatever the future might bring, the cards are certainly stacked against the orthodox party, Professor Turner suggested. After all, progressivist types often use secular institutions to carry out their agendas. Orthodox types, on the other hand, have to establish parachurch outfits to carry out their work. Reinforcing the point, Neuhaus said, "In other words, since progressives have CBS, why do they need the Christian Broadcasting Network?"

Hunter admitted that "the big variable that I understate, but not intentionally, is the nature of the state, the power and autonomy of the secular state. The state is not naked. It implicitly embodies a kind of moral vision that is more sympathetic with the progressivist wing." Chalk up two big advantages for the progressivists.

In his prediction of the Protestant future, Roof played down cultural contestation and played up mainline moderation. "The future is going to be very voluntaristic. The new voluntarism is much more, as Robert Handy said, subjective. You get vegetarian charismatic Episcopalians and nonvegetarian charismatic Episcopalians and nonvegetarian noncharismatic Episcopalians and Southern Baptists dabbling in New Thought and Lake Wobegon Lutherans and so on. The future will be terribly accommodating. It will capture the folk elements in the tradition, with the people expressing themselves in rich symbols. But some aspects of an accommodating religion are not very good."

Roof recalled some musings in the *Wall Street Journal* on the funny business that marketing religion can produce—the Mac-Church for the middle-class masses, RC Classic for the traditionalists, RC Light for the breezy, and RC Free for the liberation types.

"The groups in the center—Methodists, Lutherans, and Baptists, for example—will play a pivotal position in defining the shape of the future. These are the groups on the Protestant landscape that have some kind of balance between close communal attachments and yet an individualistic ethic. Episcopalians, Presbyterians, and United Church of Christ members have largely accommodated to a radically individualistic culture and have very weak communal attachments. Many of the newer conservative denominational groups have stronger communal ties but offer less of a chance for individuals to develop their own point of view."

Hunter, stating his view of the Protestant future, directed the conversation once again toward the Kulturkampf. He believed and hoped that the most extreme expressions of the struggle—abortion-clinic bombings, for instance—would not increase. Neuhaus responded that "that is contingent upon whether pro-life people see they have a chance of winning the abortion debate. If right-to-life forces feel that they are going to prevail in the courts, more or less, they will see the bombing as counterproductive."

Like a good Lutheran, Meg Madson of the American Lutheran Church expressed a wish for a Protestant future with a new appropriation of the Lutheran two-kingdoms doctrine. Such a position "would say that in moral-political-social debate, it is not permissible for the church to endorse policy programs or agendas. Also it would say that in this life our job is simply to take care of other people. And lastly it would say that the resouces we have as Christians are reason and the ability to compromise, negotiate, and bring many parties into the conversation. If we could get that far, it would make a tremendous contribution to the problems that Professor Hunter and others identify."

The afternoon's discussion ended with a comment by Hunter: "There is a large middle within the oldline that has not gone along with the leadership and that is increasingly vocal. It's happening, but I have not seen much documentation on it or heard much discussion of it. Unfortunately, 'the middle does not have a mailing list' for the most part."

It could be that sociologist Hunter was therein confessing how media-dependent his sociological analysis is. For the "loudest voices," which sociology can easily hear, are usually loud because they have been amplified by the media. Sometimes, however, the voices that are the loudest are not actually the most important voices.

A DEFENSE OF THE MAINLINE

The third part of the conference, which took place on Tuesday morning, was built around Thomas Derr's paper. Neuhaus introduced the paper as a "helpful explanation of the misunderstood—or it may be alternatively described as a desperate defense of the indefensible."

Very much awake, even at that early hour, Derr noted that "A hostile guest who appeared on Bill Buckley's television program once said that the hardest thing about it all was surviving Buckley's introduction."

Having eased the pain with laughter, Derr proceeded to note that "In the grand design of this conference I was hired to be the cheerleader for mainline Protestantism. The trouble is that academics make rotten cheerleaders for anything. With our thousand qualifications, we kill even that which we love." Still, Derr led on, qualifications and all.

He began by outlining three prescriptions for mainline Protestantism. First, the mainline should continue its activist, public tradition. It should continue to be an "autonomous community sprung from Christian faith" speaking unashamedly in public out of its religious convictions. Second, the mainline should, in response to imperatives from Christian theology, be more open toward other churches, nations, and peoples. And third, the mainline should pursue theological renewal.

Neuhaus was anxious to affirm Derr's first prescription. But first he footnoted. "The other day I came across a charming thing in the

Didache about the second-century true prophet/false prophet problem in Christianity. There were all kinds of people traveling around claiming that they were prophets and that they had received special visions. So the Didache gives a very firm rule of thumb as to how to tell true prophets from false prophets: if they stay more than three days, they are false prophets. Of course today all of our churches have prophets-in-residence and career tracks for prophets." Then he affirmed more seriously that "The issue of the public stance of the mainline or oldline is one that I wholeheartedly affirm. I intended *The Naked Public Square* to be an appeal to the mainline to resume its culturally formative tasks. It was not a dismissal of the mainline. It was an urgent call for the mainline, which has been so important to the American republican tradition and the whole understanding of public virtue and public discourse, to play again that role."

Mainline Pluralism?

Willimon worried about the mainline's claiming that it is pluralistic when in fact it is not acting pluralistically. "We mainliners do not believe in pluralism. We are willing to affirm you as long as you do not become fanatical or a world-withdrawing sectarian. And we are willing to talk to Marc Tannenbaum because he talks like us. But we're inclined to dismiss an Orthodox Jew on the grounds that he's losing track of the most significant task of religion, which mainliners define as propping up this wonderful nation. We believe in pluralism only to the extent that we can draw the boundaries. And when you become irrational—according to our definition of rationality—then you are out of bounds, and we don't want to talk to you. Of course that isn't real pluralism."

One of the places Willimon noticed the mainline's lack of plurality was in its public witness. "What does involvement with the world mean?" he wondered. "What does significant action mean? It means, according to Professor Derr's paper, speaking to the world. It is talk with the world. If you mention political involvement in my church, the United Methodist Church, it means writing resolutions to people in power. That is how the church is involved with the world. Derr suggests that it is the duty of the mainline to keep speaking to the world, giving people in power significant advice which then gives the church a reason for being in the first place. The call for mainline church autonomy is a noble call, but how do you do that? It seems like the minute we start worrying about the autonomy and integrity of the church, someone yells 'sectarian withdrawal!'

Because it is assumed that the duty of the church, the main purpose of the church, is to help undergird this nation-state."

Willimon concluded, "I heard Jerry Falwell on TV a few months ago on a Sunday morning talk about save-a-baby homes. He said we do not have a right to say anything about abortion if all we do is point to some pregnant fifteen-year-old and say, 'Tough luck. You've got to bear this child.' If we do not put our money and our efforts into backing up that kind of tough decision, we are being hypocritical. Falwell was saying, 'Send your money to the save-a-baby homes.' And I said, 'Amen.' You'd never hear that in my church, because we prefer to be a voice, rather than a body, a creative community where tough ethical stands are comprehensible."

Ed Dobson could not resist the opportunity presented. He inquired, "Will, did you send your money?"

No, replied Willimon, but "I said Amen. I was a voice."

Marsden made things sober again by noting another area in which the mainline is not particularly pluralistic. "There is an intolerance of pluralism in the oldline churches. The best example is in their view of public education. Protestant education started out as intolerant of Catholic education, and it controlled the public schools. Since then it has insisted that there not be alternative school systems. My impression is that mainline Protestants are almost universally committed to that, and opposed to tax money going to the parochial school systems that Catholics, Lutherans, some evangelicals and fundamentalists have. That is where the court cases are coming up. The mainline always lines up on one side of those cases because it still has this illusion that the public educational system is its system." The mainline attitude toward public schooling even carried over into higher education, said Marsden. "Mainline churches have gotten rid of their colleges and universities during this century. This is seldom noticed. One of the reasons evangelicals and fundamentalists probably have a much better future than the mainline is that the mainline doesn't have any schools anymore. They have had the illusion that the public schools would support them."

As always, Dean Kelley was ready and waiting to challenge a prevailing stereotype. "With reference to disillusionment with the public schools and to the voucher system, I will reveal a small secret from inside the ecumenical movement. There is a great deal of disillusionment with the public schools. I think there will be a policy favoring something like the voucher plan or tuition-tax credits coming forth from the gargantuan machinery of policy statements one of these years."

Having undermined one stereotype, Kelley was prepared to question the assertion that the mainline is not pluralistic. "I staffed a task force that worked for four years on the development of an ecumenical observance of the Bicentennial in 1976. At one point we brought a magnificent resolution to the executive committee of the National Council of Churches to lift up this occasion from a Christian perspective. We had carefully avoided an overenthusiastic endorsement of the social structure and had come up with a legitimate pride in its basic ideals and concepts. But the executive committee, which was trying to include many voices of Christian groups, was immediately torn by cross fire from two groups within itself. The white hierarchs insisted that it was much too negative, and the black members said that they didn't see anything to celebrate. Between those two it was very difficult to maintain a sane, stable course. But it was and is worth a try."

The mainline is trying, sincerely trying, to be pluralistic, said Kelley, but that might be part of its troubles.

Well, perhaps oldline leaderships are trying to be inclusive with regard to each other, but even so, they seem to be excluding "mainstream America," said Richard Hutcheson. "The term *mainstream* has relevance. Historically, the mainline churches have been churches speaking to and for the mainstream of America. It was always other American denominations that were radically confrontational in their stance toward society. One of the problems with the confrontational attitude recently adopted by mainline leadership is the danger that it renders them no longer mainstream. Historically, being mainline has meant being both critical and responsible. Unfortunately, there is a real danger right now of mainline establishments marginalizing themselves from mainstream America."

What really is at stake in the marginalization of mainline leadership? "The character of the Christian community," said Neuhaus. "Leadership may feel that by being marginalized it is confirmed in its consciousness of itself as being prophetic. But what is at stake is the ecclesiological question—namely, How do the people of God participate in the church's public witness? Whether one does it in the Roman Catholic terms of collegiality or the Quaker terms of the sense of the meeting or whatever, if the ecclesiological presupposition were attended to, the leadership would not find itself so marginalized. That would not be a compromise of its prophetic ministry but rather an exercise in fidelity to its commitment to the body of Christ, the church."

One means of public witness the church should not attempt is the means of accommodationism, Neuhaus urged. The mainline leadership should not tailor its public witness to fit new-class tastes and opinions. Nor should mainline leaders fill the order placed by the old business class or by mainstream America. Neuhaus maintained that the church should be the church first and last, and never the lackey chaplain of a class, group, or interest.

Nancy Ammerman was bothered by the talk of the American mainstream. "When I hear talk about the church returning to its place representing the mainstream and being the church of and for the mainstream, I become very worried. Because the mainstream often translates into those who have been the dominant classes and who have excluded those outside their boundaries." Theologically, she said, she could say Amen to letting the church be the church. Sociologically, she sadly concluded, she recognizes the inherent tendency of churches to draw boundaries around themselves that clearly coincide with social divides.

With a devious grin, Weigel commented on the fate of the Protestant smile. "Over the past day and a half, the Protestant smile has been replaced by a furrowed brow. I was wondering what is going on here. Suddenly, it dawned on me. You guys really have believed that you were in charge of this show for two hundred years. That's astounding! Well, let me tell you something: you weren't. At least not entirely. The mainline was not solely responsible for bringing American society to this cultural moment, and it will certainly not be solely responsible for taking us into the future."

Weigel's realism assumed a genuine pluralism. But pluralism is something mainline Protestantism does not exhibit, remarked James Hunter, concurring with Willimon's earlier comment. "I have a profound sense that the mainline still does not recognize that there is somebody else around. This is a kind of imperialistic posture that neglects other groups. But the public square is not naked. It has been filled by other voices," he said, mixing metaphors.

"It seems to me," Marsden remarked, "that the main thing that has been said this morning is that what's wrong with mainline Protestantism is that it's politically liberal-Democratic. We have used code words, such as 'new class,' in order to say that. But that doesn't tell me much. The crucial point is what criteria we have to criticize the churches' social-political involvement. Can anyone come up with criteria that are critical of both the neoconservative agenda and the liberal-Democratic agenda? Or is the bottom line that if a church is neoconservative, it is OK, but if it is liberal-Democratic, it isn't? We have to get beyond that."

Gently and fraternally, Neuhaus asked Marsden to name names, because he said he hadn't heard anyone arguing for a neoconservative church. Marsden declined, but asked if the morning's discussion contained any criticism of "the neoconservative agenda."

With strong feeling Neuhaus replied: "I'm a democrat—upper case and lower case. But I am concerned first of all with the character of the church as a community and secondly—and I don't think there is anything neoconservative about this—with the church's cultural-formative role in revitalizing the American democratic experiment. I don't think this is party- or policy-specific."

"If the church is to be the church, it can't be predictable about where it is going to come out on political issues," Marsden asserted.

"Amen!" agreed Neuhaus.

Thinking about the Third World

Some within the world of mainline Protestantism might boast of their pluralistic and open style when in fact they are enforcing a rigid orthodoxy. One item in this orthodoxy's system of belief concerns a "Third World mystique." Rabbi Novak elaborated.

"The Derr paper indicates something extremely disturbing in mainline American Protestantism at the present time—what I would call the 'Third World mystique.' Mainline Protestantism especially is now in the process of a rather guilty self-examination of the church's easy capitulations to the powers that be. The most glaring example is the example of the German church, except for the Confessing Church. Indeed, that does require soul-searching. But there is the notion that the church will resume its purity in the face of a hostile government when it is a minority of purity over against a hostile government engaged in imperialism and so on. Although one can go to the other extreme and write a blank check to American capitalism, there seems to be this Third World mystique that says because Protestantism was so culture-positive in the past and that led to all kinds of corruptions, its mission should now be antisociety, antigovernment, that that is how it will regain its purity. This is, with no disrespect to his memory, the Dietrich Bonhoeffer syndrome." American mainline Protestantism should not "automatically assume that Western society is corrupt and evil and that its task is to be 'prophetic' by calling for society's downfall," Novak urged.

Madson leapt to Novak's defense. "His point is accurate. If one goes to the World Council of Churches or the National Council of Churches, one finds there is no diversity within the Third World speakers who are on the platforms. It is ideologically uniform, and it is not very self-critical. Western civilization is seen as the oppressor civilization."

Yes and no, cautioned Kelley. "There is a lot of foolish faddism and sentimental romanticism that goes on in the ecumenical world. But it is also the case that ecumenism's problems are often the result of trying to do something very difficult—include groups that are not represented around this Princeton Club table." Kelley then spoke of the luxury of the conference's relatively homogeneous group of participants—homogeneous, that is, with respect to socioeconomic class and academic background. That is a luxury not often enjoyed in mainline-ecumenical settings, he noted. "Proponents of ecumenism don't always include others wisely, and they don't always do it well, but they try to do it! Many of the things seen by outside critics as excesses or errors are the results of this effort."

Novak had not actually completed his statement on the Third World. The second time around he was very specific. "One of the things that is very, very shocking to many people in the Jewish community about Protestantism is how little concern you show for your own persecuted minorities. If we hear anywhere that there is a threat to kill a Jew, we have a rally, we start petitions, and we get everything going. And yet we hear about Christians being persecuted in the Third World and we do not understand why Protestants are not crying out."

Novak's comment prompted Willimon to recall an incident. "Somebody from 475 Riverside Drive was bragging to me the other day about how wonderful it was to be in New York because he gets to have a bag lunch every week with a different UN delegation. He said that he met with a group from Mozambique last week and it was just marvelous. And I asked why that would be marvelous, because he was meeting with people who are persecuting our people, Christians, over there."

Dennis Campbell appreciated the more ecclesiological turn in the conversation. It prompted him to delineate one of the Third World's theological contributions to the church. "My experience with Christians in the Third World indicates that they are very much interested in Christological issues," he began. "The identity of Christ and its implications are very important to them. But when liberal American Protestants look at the Third World, they really don't want to engage such issues because of the embarrassment of particularity. We should not say that there is a kind of romanticism about the Third World and therefore we shouldn't be interested. We should be very much interested in the particularity of the religious claims being made there."

As it turned out, Derr was not advocating that the mainline churches pick up and push a hard Third World agenda. But the fact that the mere mention of the Third World in his paper elicited such strong and interesting comments suggests that the Third World issue is indeed a part of the Protestant Kulturkampf that Hunter had described.

To Endorse or Not to Endorse

James Reichley got into a discussion of the mainline support for the Humphrey-Hawkins Act of the 1970s, which he suggested had damaged mainline credibility and divided its household. Neuhaus wondered whether the incident offered any lessons. "Would it be a useful rule of thumb," he asked, "that the church should not commit itself publicly to policies or positions that are empirically falsifiable?"

"On a prudential basis the church does not need to stay away from what is falsifiable," Himmelfarb said. "After all, if you are an intellectual or a professor, you are invulnerable to this rule. If you are a used-car salesman or a football coach, you'd better have a record of accomplishment or people will stop buying cars from you or hiring you to coach their teams. If you are a professor at the Woodrow Wilson School at Princeton, you can say hurrah for Khomeini, hurrah for Mao Tse-tung and continue to be a professor of international relations, no matter how often your opinions are falsified."

There seemed to be a lot of agreement with Himmelfarb's point around the room. Kelley, for example, ventured that "The risk of being wrong is minimalized in the professions. University professors have to go on after they make mistakes. The clergy predict the end of the world in 1943 and yet carry on when it doesn't happen. Lawyers too insist on collecting their fee after they lose their case, and doctors after they bury the patient. So there is no reason religion should not do this." Often it is unwise for the church to endorse or oppose a candidate by name, Kelley continued. "However, the time may come when duty calls us to do that, as *Christian Century* and *Christianity and Crisis* thought it did when they wrote editorials opposing Goldwater and thereby lost their tax exemption. That's a risk the church must take," said Kelley.

Derr seconded Kelley's opinion. "If in church pronouncements you tried to avoid the risk of partisan mistakes, you will end up not saying what ought to be said at critical junctures. The question of course is the point the church's speech must become specific, and as a general rule I think it usually should not be."

Neuhaus placed on the table another means and illustration of escaping falsifiability. "As a McGovern delegate at the 1972

Democratic convention and a member of several of his advisory committees, I remember how self-evidently we used the key phrase 'constituency of conscience.' When the constituency of conscience only got thirty-four percent of the American vote, all that demonstrated to us was that conscience is always in the minority. It does not matter what the consequences are, for they can always be reinterpreted in a way that is self-serving."

At this point John Cooper objected. The issue is not falsifiability, he insisted; the issue is partisanship. "We have everywhere in our culture but the church a very clear understanding about the difference between partisan and nonpartisan. It is written in the tax code. Think tanks use it all the time. Universities use it all the time. Yet in the churches we are still worrying about whether a pastor ought to endorse a candidate, a particular public policy, or a piece of legislation from the pulpit. It is dragging Christianity through the mud by hitching its team to some secular cart. I don't know why the churches have such a hankering to be lobbying organizations."

Turner took exception with Cooper's partisanship test. Would not such a test imply that churches should not have supported the Voting Rights Act of 1965? "I don't know that we want to put ourselves in the position of saying the church may never pronounce on legislation," he mildly put it.

All of us might be missing the boat here, ventured Neuhaus. In public statements the character of the church and the consultation within the Christian community should be more formative of what church leadership does in official action and position-taking than what the law prohibits or allows in terms of partisanship. The integrity of the church—not the test of empirical falsifiability or the test of partisanship—is the most important factor in determining when and how the church will take a public stand on public issues, he contended.

A Neo-Orthodox Hegemony?

To speak about neo-orthodoxy in the context of American Protestantism is to speak about Reinhold Niebuhr. He stands as both the exemplar and the representative theologian of the neo-orthodox movement. Early on Derr claimed the neo-orthodox tradition as his own; later, quite understandably, he claimed the Niebuhrian legacy, or what he took to be the Niebuhrian legacy, as his own. Said Derr on neo-orthodoxy,

"Most of today's mainline leaders grew up when I did—in the 1950s under the sway of neo-orthodoxy. We then resented very much the term 'liberal' applied to our theology. One of my mentors, John Bennett, said that he hoped he would live long enough to see what would come after neo-orthodoxy, since neo-orthodoxy was such an all-encompassing movement. Then about ten years later he said that he had lived long enough, but he couldn't tell what it was that had come after neo-orthodoxy. That is a fair assessment of the confusion of the 1960s. At any rate, neo-orthodoxy was a dominating movement. I don't believe its forces have faded. Because of it, much of mainline leadership today would resent being called liberal theologically."

When critics assert that mainline Protestantism has "gone whoring after false gods, that it has become a camp follower of secular society," and that such is the fault of liberal theology, Derr plays his neo-orthodox card, arguing that neo-orthodoxy never did and never would let the mainline fall into that fatal trap. He assumes that a militant variety of neo-orthodoxy is alive and well on the mainline scene today.

Weigel, a Catholic, saw something very attractive in Protestant neo-orthodoxy. It might assist the mainline in its culture-forming task, he suggested, by helping it to develop "criteria for making discriminating judgments in the public arena. The values we want to forward in our common life are not simply floating in the ether. They have to be incarnated in institutions if they are going to be protected and vital in the future. This is one of the truthfulnesses and usefulnesses of neo-orthodoxy. It is the perennial reminder of the ever-present danger of gnosticism, the unfleshing of Christian moral imagination. This suggests that there are two obstacles to this new culture-forming-discriminating-criteria role of the mainline. There is a kind of liberal gnosticism that fails to distinguish between inadequate-bad-worse and can only say 'A plague on all your houses' or indiscriminately adopt the fashionable option of the moment. There is also a kind of evangelical-fundamentalist gnosticism that doesn't want to develop or is hesitant about developing discriminating criteria because it's nervous about getting polluted by the world. It thinks that too much activity in sorting out inadequate-bad-worse inevitably involves you in a theology and politics of compromise. Both of these options have a kind of unearthly quality, a gnostic quality." Though he did not say it in so many words, Weigel implied that, given neo-orthodoxy's current low ratings in American Protestantism, the hope for the development of criteria for public judgment remains no more than that—a hope.

On neo-orthodoxy Mark Silk was quite explicit. He called for a neo-orthodox-establishment future for American Protestantism.

"Do we hope for a future in continuity with names like Niebuhr, Tillich, Oxnam, and Van Dusen? Was that the great age that one might want to return to? There was probably something there that is now being missed—a set of voices that at least tried not to engage in special-interest pleading. That is a kind of establishment role. We live in a deeply antiestablishment society, which is more or less a good thing. But we also generate establishments of an informal and involuntary nature. Rather than a pluralism of many voices, what is desired is a mainline recovery of the voice of the center that adjudicated and tried to reconcile interests, that welcomed in Jews and peace-church people and tried to hear what they have to say about how we work out our common life."

Willimon did not go for all of this uncritical praise of neo-orthodoxy and Niebuhr. "Behind Tom Derr's paper and much of our conversation there is that Protestant nostalgia for the good old days of Niebuhrian hegemony over our thought. And they *were* the good old days, because in a sense we were in charge, and we could afford to be benevolent to others who we allowed into the conversation on our terms. And the terms were about politics. Reinhold Niebuhr was a tremendous help to American Protestantism in that he helped us to adjust to being powerful. He helped you to run a bank and not feel guilty about it, as a Protestant. But now we're in a changed situation. Niebuhr was not interested in the church. He didn't have to be interested because the church was strong and powerful, a sleeping giant that needed to be mobilized for the right causes. I don't see that kind of strength now in mainline Protestantism. I see a weak, dispirited group of people struggling and wondering where they stand within American society. When I hear Protestants on the left and the right discussing these things, I hear a debate over how to make the church culturally significant again—in other words, politically significant. We are not ready to discuss the character of the church, because we are much more concerned with being culturally significant. My problem is that I worship a Jew who was killed by a Caesar. All Pilate wanted was peace with justice, and it bothers me that that is all the church wants now."

Before Derr responded to Willimon's view of the establishment Niebuhr, he wanted to establish his credentials: "If I am nothing else, I am a Niebuhrian." With that made clear, he continued. "In the heyday of neo-orthodoxy I do not think that Niebuhr thought that he was in charge or that he represented a party that was in charge. He was into professional agitation. I wouldn't have thought he represented the stance of those who had power."

With that Tom Derr ended his spirited defense of mainline Protestantism in America. It was a defense that answered some questions and raised others. It also served to set forth a future of American Protestantism that is very believable. And finally, it prepared the way for the discussion of Thomas Oden's paper, which proposes a future for the mainline that differs radically from the mainline's present course.

A NEW REFORMATION?

Oden had been assigned to kick off the New Reformation. It would have been understandable had he approached this awesome task somewhat timidly, but in fact his approach was hardly timid. And, quoting John Wesley, he counseled those around the conference table to avoid timidity as well. "Wesley had a phrase that he used—'Smite me friendly.' And I welcome the punch. I want to hear your critique."

Oden proceeded to talk about what it was he wanted critiqued.

"My premise is that we do not have to invent a new strategy, a new theological approach. Everything that is in fact required for the future care of American Protestantism is already offered in the classical Christian tradition. The irony is that the future of Protestantism, as I envision it, is a catholic future and a recovery.

"There is a soteriological metaphor that was often employed by the older Protestant dogmaticians that said that salvation in Christ is as an inheritance given but often unappropriated. In other words, it is as if I have a check in the bank already but I have not cashed it and I have not even acknowledged that it is there. What I am talking about is the deposit of tradition that is there but unacknowledged, unused, unreferred to."

The classical Christian tradition is locked up or out, so to speak, by the chauvinism of modernity, Oden continued. Classical Christianity is also hampered by an American-Protestant problem. "It has been a Protestant habit to rule out everything between the New Testament and the modern day. But it is also a very American habit to rule out anything that does not look new and fresh." So the tradition is kept hidden while the American Protestant churches suffer. Yes, Oden reiterated, "The church is really suffering enormously from its lack of leadership."

"It may seem as if I am defiantly premodern in my attitude," Oden continued, "but I do not feel that way at all. I feel myself to be postcritical, postmodern. I am extremely antimodern, but that does not mean premodern. I'm after the recovery of a living tradition. What I am saying is reactionary. I want to own up to that term, because my position is a reaction to and is strongly determined by the limits of the present visions of political and ecclesial life. But the term I most want to own is *orthodoxy*. It has been the hardest for me to own, because I come right out of the center of the liberal tradition."

Oden's liberal credentials are indeed impressive. As a "movement theologian," he went from pacificism to self-conscious socialism to existentialism to psychotherapy—and now, to orthodoxy.

Oden wanted to get something straight—the definition of *believable*. "I would like to reinterpret the term *believable*. I would like to shift it away from a calculus of probability. In other words, if I had to put my credit card out here and bet my chips, I wouldn't bet on my vision of Protestantism as a probability hypothesis. But I think it is very important to keep in mind that the Holy Spirit is active in the future of the Church. That is the wild card. The Holy Spirit is clearly going to be guiding the Christian community through the hazards of postmodern, postcritical, postsecular culture. And so I would want to put a very strong emphasis on the classical doctrine of providence, which Catholics and Protestants share. And although I know a priori arguments drive modern consciousness up the wall, I would want to rely very strongly on an a priori argument about the Holy Spirit. What I mean is that I want to rely on the Spirit prior to any empirical data gathering. This entails an assumption about the nature of God and the providential care of God for creation—an assumption that the redemptive purposes of God will be worked out regardless of our moral inadequacies, lack of political wisdom, and lack of knowledge."

At that juncture Oden responded to Derr's three prescriptions for mainline Protestantism—social activism, openness, and ecumenism. First he tackled social activism.

"The great need in American Protestantism's social engagement is not for a new stratagem of political consensus but for a recovery of the doctrine of vocation. If we could get hold of that one point, fundamental changes might occur in our society. Clergy should preach the Word and administer the sacraments in such a way as to make faith active in love and to enable faith to be perceived in relation to specific lay vocational challenges. This is where the political strength of Protestantism has been and will continue to be. But today I do not hear people talking about vocation."

Second, Oden addressed openness. "The forms of openness that I find, for example, at 475 Riverside Drive are extremely limited. Inclusivism has been used as a club against those offering a differing view and vision of the church." The real challenge, he suggested, is for those in mainline Protestantism to enter into dialogue with those who differ radically from the mainline—conservative Jews, say, or Islamic fundamentalists. "Radical openness," according to Oden, is what is needed.

And third, Oden on ecumenism: "I am coming more and more to a sense of the dismal failure of the ecumenical movement. The organizational ecumenicity that we have seen is totally dull and totally uninteresting." But there is potential for a new ecumenical movement between centrist Protestants and the evangelical tradition. "That is an ecumenical dialogue that has so far to go. Every time it is even broached I find there is tremendous resistance to it in the Consultation on Church Union circles."

Next on the Oden agenda was a confession and a charge: "I see the problem of American Protestantism from the vantage point of the education of its clergy. I see my own failure as a teacher, the failure of my own theological school, the failure of my own denomination, the failure of the ecumenical movement that I have been earnestly committed to for over thirty years. A fundamental reversal is needed. The best place to begin this is in the ordination committee, the place where there is in fact some reasonable control over candidates for ordination. Let's hope that eventually bishops can be elected who share these concerns. I am not thinking just of the election of bishops but generally of the leadership of the clergy. If we had a courageous quality of episcopacy, a teaching episcopacy, that stood with integrity in the apostolic succession, then we might have a believable future."

Does Withdrawal Mean Retreat?

Oden then advanced to a very important question: Exactly how should a postcritical orthodoxy confront the public square?

"The postcritical orthodox Christian community must learn how to pray. Intercession is the most important thing that it can do. We must seek freedom to be ourselves, to proclaim our witness. And I think that is a worldwide task. I think that we have a responsibility to proclaim that message in places where it is not possible to proclaim. I am talking about the Soviet Union, China, and many other places around the world. And especially we are being called to transform our own communities into places that make a more plausible and vital contribution to the social process."

That means withdrawal, Oden stated. In fact, he urged that the withdrawal of the Christian community from the public square is absolutely necessary. "I find myself for the time being in the withdrawalist mode. I'm in the Christ-against-culture slot of Richard Niebuhr's scheme. Niebuhr's prototypes for that were Tertullian and Tolstoy. I do not have a great sense of affinity for either, but for the withdrawalist motif—the Amish are an example of this—I feel a great sense of affinity, because of what I regard as the demonic character of modernity. It is deceptive; it is self-deceptive. It has a consistently self-deceptive character. Before we are prepared to make a transformationist initiative—and I don't think we are, and I don't think we are going to be for twenty years—we have got to undergo the ascetic disciplines, the disciplines that will be required of a transformationist movement. John Wesley is an example of one who did that in the eighteenth century. In him there were both the withdrawalist and the transformationist themes, but the transformationist themes came much, much later. A lot of what happens when we are calling ourselves transformationists is really what Richard Niebuhr called accommodationist. We are just accommodating. And we have seen too much of that."

Willimon didn't like the looks of the withdrawal mode that Oden was beginning to fashion. "The current political discussion," he argued, "tells the church, 'You've either got to get in and play ball according to our rules or you've got to withdraw.' When I grew up the the 1960s, they were always telling us to get out of the church and into the real world. That immediately set up the conversation in such a way that anything we found in the church wouldn't be real. The point of a lot of the Church Fathers was, 'Come into the church, come into the real world, and get out of the fake world. We want to bring you in so that you can see things for what they are and call them by their proper names, not as the world calls them.' That is not withdrawing. That is simply saying, 'By God, we are going to define the world. We will define it for you. And we will define it not simply in our intellectual life but also in the kind of life we create together.' That is being intensely involved, but in our own way."

Furthermore, Willimon thought he detected a glaring inconsistency in Oden's case. "In a sense, Tom is adopting the world's ways by saying that the future depends on the power in the church flowing from the top down and on getting good people who can manage it well."

Dennis Campbell interjected, "I don't hear Professor Oden saying that at all."

Willimon was quick to respond to Dean Campbell, "Well, you want to believe that theological education is the significant key to the future."

But Campbell was just as quick to respond by pointing out the crucial difference between the teaching authority that Oden was calling for and the hierarchical authority that Willimon was speaking of. Oden was talking about the proper pedagogical role of the clergy, Campbell said, not a hierarchical-bureaucratic model of church management.

Neuhaus remarked that Willimon seemed to be pushing the church to enter, perhaps for the first time, the pluralistic competition of the American public square with a Christian definition of reality. Up until now, he contended, the church has been translating Christian language into secular language to assure all of its relevance. But now Willimon was saying that "if you want to talk to the church, you translate into the church's language," said Neuhaus. That is really aggressive; in fact, it is the opposite of withdrawal, and yet it might make some sort of withdrawal necessary for the Church to retrieve its Christian language—or its "cultural-linguistic tradition," as Yale's George Lindbeck puts it. Neuhaus concluded, "It's a catch-22 proposition. If you don't have the language to assert, you have no role in the competition. You literally have nothing to say."

James Turner noticed that "somewhere in the low forties" of Oden's propositions, "where the essay gets more specific about the relationship of the church to the political arena, patristic exegeses fall off. Suddenly we have Reformation exegeses. I wonder if that symbolizes a cleavage between an older Catholic tradition and some kind of Reformation innovation."

No cleavage was intended, nor did he intend to overemphasize Luther and Calvin, replied Oden. Then he referred to parts of the catholic tradition that he found particularly instructive on matters of church and society: "I find myself greatly instructed by Gregory the Great, who was an enormously effective diplomat in his time and delivered the Christian tradition of the medieval world almost single-handedly under enormous threats. I have great admiration for the political skills of people who were committed to the tradition of orthodoxy. If you look behind that, I have even greater admiration for the period of martyrdom, in which there was a marginality and disenfranchisement of the church. We have a lot to learn from that, particularly if we have to face either fascist or Marxist tyrannies within our society, which could happen in the next hundred to two hundred years. We might have to learn a great deal from the second and third centuries very quickly."

Campbell was still uneasy with this withdrawal business. He wanted to get very specific: "What would it mean for a tenured professor in a university divinity school to take withdrawal seriously?

Would it not drive professors and teachers to the point of utter frustration? The institutions we serve are given to us by God in Christ. I do believe that. If that is the case, then we have inherited them, problematic as they are. Somehow we have got to learn how to serve them in our day. What we ought to be about in our day is aggressive entry into the public arena. I think we ought to be taking increasingly aggressive postures of proclamation."

Oden concurred in principle but not in strategy: "My intention was to speak of a *relative* withdrawal that seeks to prepare itself for a more profound engagement. Accommodationism in the church has been so rife for so long that a relative retrenching from that is absolutely necessary if we are going to discover our own identity and center in a new way."

Then Oden spoke personally: "I have decided it is extremely important for me to stay where I am—to hang in there, even under great difficulties." Again, in surveying classical Christianity, Oden sees vocation, even personally, as the key to the church's engagement with the world.

Orthodoxy Today

Several conferees thought they spotted problems in Oden's approach to orthodoxy. Meg Madson was the first: "The Oden approach assumes unanimity on what the apostolic tradition comprises. This is precisely the ecumenical problem. I am mindful of what Karl Barth said—that the New Testament is the mother of all heresy. It has also been noted that heresies have been with the church from the very beginning and that there is no pristine period or time when everyone concurred in their beliefs." Neuhaus added that the Vincentian formula—that which has been believed by the everyone in the church at all times and in all places—might be nothing but an illusion.

Oden brushed aside Neuhaus's aside and replied to Madson's comment. "We do have a period of history in which very, very careful attention was given to drawing a line between orthodoxy and heresy. That was an extremely complex process. Those decisions were in fact consensual. They are ecumenical. I am talking about the seven ecumenical councils as, on the whole, representing the consensus of orthodoxy." He added that "Lutheranism on the whole has accepted much of the language of that ecumenical period."

Neuhaus overruled Oden's qualification: "All of it."

Madson reinserted it: "Some of it."

Neuhaus remained insistent: "All of it!"

Amid the chuckles of the non-Lutherans around the table, the argument was abandoned.

Tom Derr was the next to tangle with Oden's orthodoxy. He began by recalling that "in the early 1960s there was a story by and about Roger Shinn. He was in a small discussion group which also included a Catholic moral theologian. Shinn asked the theologian why there was so little in the fulsome compendium of Catholic moral teaching on the race issue. The reply was that it was a subdivision of moral theology that only now, in the course of the ages, was beginning to be developed. Shinn said, 'Nonsense. You are thinking about it now because there are Negroes in the streets.'"

Derr proceeded to ask, "Why does feminism now appear in Oden's paper, when one would have thought that the weight of the apostolic tradition was against it? It puts a dark suspicion in my feeble mind. I wonder if this item on the agenda wasn't really invoked by modern circumstances, whether Oden hasn't gone back to the apostolic tradition on a kind of treasure hunt to see what he could find to defend it."

Oden went on the defensive. "Why feminism now? It seems to me that God's Spirit is doing something special in our time with respect to calling women. God has always called women, but calling women into sacred ministry is a new appropriation of what I understand to be the original deposit of faith that has indeed been misunderstood for nineteen centuries.

"In the nineteenth century a substantial exegesis went on concerning the Pauline passages that have often been taken by this consensual tradition to be normative. It determined that Paul was not in fact rejecting the ministry of women in the passage in 1 Corinthians; rather, he was rejecting and attacking the principle of the usurpation of authority and using women as an example.

"So I still want to hold to a principle of John Henry Newman—namely, that the deposit of faith is fully given in the beginning and requires a developmental process as well. For example, on slavery. Why did it take the church so long to realize the moral evil of slavery? Well, the Holy Spirit worked in such a way that it was more possible in the eighteenth century than previously. But that's mystery. We do not know why the Spirit works."

Neuhaus was unconvinced. "What are the relevant criteria in discerning the Spirit's work? People who say the Spirit is moving are also saying the Spirit is moving with regard to homosexuality, with regard to abortion, and so on."

In answer, Oden went back to the idea of orthodoxy as the

Vincentian process, which takes years—even centuries—to achieve even a rough consensus of Christian belief.

Oden's appeal to the Holy Spirit dissatisfied Rabbi Novak. "In rabbinic tradition," he said, "there is a very important concept—that 'The Torah is no longer in heaven.' Torah came from heaven, direct from heaven, but is in the hands of human beings to judge. What that doctrine means is that one cannot invoke the Holy Spirit in our tradition. One can pray for its guidance, but ultimately one's argument has to be based on the hard evidence of the tradition itself." Novak, it might be said, was calling for more evidence, "hard evidence."

Ed Dobson loosened things up a bit. "Basically," he joked, "I thought the Church Fathers were Billy Graham and Jerry Falwell." The laughter that followed did not indicate agreement. But Dobson had something more serious on his mind. He tended to equate orthodoxy with the center, and he was not interested in being in the center.

"As a fundamentalist," he said, "I am not in the center. And I have no desire to prove that I am in the center of something so that you will accept me. If you are committed to confronting the culture and changing the culture, as fundamentalism is, you really don't care what people think about you." He recalled having appeared on the Phil Donahue show some time ago and having been booed by the audience. He claimed that this was a wonderful experience—and that it would be for anyone who truly desired to confront and change the culture.

"But Phil is not the culture—yet," Neuhaus interjected. Furthermore, he postulated that Dobson was doing a "wee bit of posturing," for fundamentalists are indeed culturally centrist according to Hadden, Roof, and others. Dobson refused to repent for the venial sin of posturing, but he did admit that fundamentalism is increasingly tempted by the lure of the respectability of the cultural center.

Dobson's comment led Oden to admit that "listening responsively to the whole of the consensual tradition is really what I am about. I think that is not very far from the fundamentalists in their single-minded attempt to listen to the Bible. What I am trying to do is listen to the Bible, yes. But I'm also trying to listen to the Bible through the writings of those who listened to the Bible best. I'm talking about Gregory of Nazianzus. How long has it been since you read him? I think the Southern Baptists at Liberty University could do very, very well by reading a little bit of Gregory and all of the other Cappadocian Fathers."

Silk put the conversation on a different track. "The medieval project had to confront the many conflicting voices in the Christian tradition that were already present by the middle of the eleventh century. I do not think that among those doing theology then there was any sense of the apostolic tradition providing a single clear answer. The medieval theological achievement is remarkable, among other reasons, for its rich theological diversity."

Neuhaus extended Silk's point by stating that the medieval achievement had to do with "sorting things out." For despite all of the theological diversity of that era, all of the theologians, according to Neuhaus, saw themselves as part of a single conversation, though not of a single viewpoint or a single school of thought. That conversation, in which all of the participants are at least acquainted with the same points of reference, is the conversation of orthodoxy.

Oden seconded Neuhaus's opinion. "Orthodoxy is a diversity. This is really what is magnificent to me about orthodoxy, not its homogeneity. Homogeneity is not what is exciting about orthodoxy. Its flexibility, its ability to copulate with this culture and that culture, to stay alive and stay rooted in the tradition is absolutely amazing to me. It is radically capable of moving in and out of cultures."

Then Neuhaus reinforced Oden's opinion. "People are turning to orthodoxy not because they have found a conservative impulse in themselves but they have found liberalism so stifling, so conservative in the negative sense. Orthodoxy is ever so much more adventuresome intellectually, historically, conceptually, and in every possible way. It is really an irony—liberation by tradition."

Weigel was ready to sketch, in rough form, a believable future. "I think we have got a believable future here in which there is a kind of ecumenism that focuses primarily on first principles—not on questions of church polity, important as they are; nor on common public policy concerns, important as they are. In this ecumenism we genuinely try to deal with the fear on the left that a return to the great sources of the past is an accommodation to know-nothingism, and the fear on the right that there may be things that have happened in the Christian church since the eighteenth century that have not been all that bad. The goal of this new ecumenism of first principles is not going to be to get everyone to sign off on the same set of propositional formulations. The goal would be what John Courtney Murray referred to thirty years ago as the great accomplishment of achieving disagreement. If we could get from cacophony to disagreement, which would mean that we all are at least operating with the same reference points, that would not be bad." Call it, he suggested, what John Cardinal O'Connor calls it—"dynamic orthodoxy."

Mainline seminaries, Campbell lamented, are not ready for—indeed they usually resist—a dynamic orthodoxy. "With regard to theological education, Professor Oden's paper is right on target. The kind of self-critical reflection that Tom is exemplifying in this paper is absolutely essential to the so-called mainline theological education faculties in this country. In certain places it is beginning to take place, but I think it is by no means generalized. We are still very much in a situation where the theological faculties are convinced that they are right and that what they are doing is good. Basically, they are self-satisfied."

Campbell related an incident that underlines the poverty of mainline theology in the seminaries and churches. "In the Rocky Mountain Conference of the United Methodist Church there was a brouhaha about the tests for ordination and inclusive language about God, particularly the equation of Creator-Redeemer-Sustainer and Father-Son-Holy Spirit. What struck me about that was that there was no capacity in the Board of Ordained Ministry there to deal theologically with that question. The only resources they had were contemporary cultural discussions, particularly from the feminist point of view. So the bankruptcy of mainline theology and theological education now comes full circle to the boards and committees being unable to do their given tasks. The future of mainline Protestantism will depend on the ability of the church to recognize that it is the job of all ordained persons to take upon themselves the authority for teaching and that this teaching must not be a matter of how the individual may feel at the time but must have some reference to the tradition." Or, Campbell might have said, to an orthodoxy.

Turner then turned to Oden and said, "As I have listened to you expand your thoughts in this essay and your responses to people, a lot of the themes seem to hang together. You want a return to, if I can misuse Leavis's phrase, the Great Tradition, in some sense, as the major source of our theological reflection—particularly the pre-Reformation parts of that tradition which you tend to regard as having been lost in the last century or two of Protestantism. You want bishops to take a stronger role in ensuring sound doctrine. You want a clergy that will undertake the theological renewal of the church and a laity whose role will essentially be to pray. You urge a clearly differentiated role between clergy and laity. And you want a church that would have some effective means for taking care of heresy. Those things sound familiar to me. Now I do not think that you are trying to tell us the believable future of American Protestantism is Roman Catholicism. But why not? How would you distinguish your position from a rather traditional Roman Catholic position—one that is willing, as Catholics now are, to take serious theological account of Luther, Calvin, and so on?"

"What I am looking for is not fundamentally distinguishable from Roman Catholicism," Oden replied. "It is the classical Christian tradition. My intuitions are fundamentally catholic, but less Roman Catholic than ancient-ecumenical. It is inclusive of both East and West. I am particularly grasped by minds in the East. I have a problem with the exclusion of women from the priesthood in the Roman Catholic tradition, although that has yet to be played out. Those are some of the distinctions that I would want to press."

Would It Make a Difference?

The next part of the conference conversation dealt with the what-if question. Elliot Wright put it this way: "Let's say that a significant part of the mainline would take Oden's theology seriously and try to recover what it means to pray and what it means to be a community of God's people. It reforms its house—and I don't mean it just has a reorganization of its bureaucracy. But it reforms the curriculum of the seminaries first. It is, let's say, very self-conscious about this undertaking—with an idea that down the road there might be the possibility of some reformist movement in the society at large. My question would be: What difference does that make in a pluralistic society?"

Neuhaus joined Wright in wondering if a theologically serious church might do nothing more than provide one more item or option or choice on the cultural cafeteria line. He quoted an archbishop of the Church of England as saying, in all seriousness, that "the mission of the Church of England is to keep alive the religious alternative for those interested in that sort of thing."

"The difference," Oden suggested, "would be made in the world of vocation—among people cleaning up these tables, working as policemen out there, constructing buildings, even teaching theology. This used to be central to Protestant teaching, but it is no longer so important. That does make a tremendous difference. That is a part of what accounted for the vitality of nineteenth-century Protestantism and its impact on the American scene. The difference is not necessarily made in public policy. Forget about public policy. Public policy is relatively unimportant in my view. I know that I'm exaggerating here. If Wright is asking a pragmatic and utilitarian question about how you affect public policy, I would say that we should let somebody else answer that question. That is not my question."

Neuhaus took a stab at Wright's question and suggested that the difference would be made in the integrity of the church as community. Such integrity, as far as Neuhaus is concerned, involves, in part, submission to an external authority. "Theological discourse," he continued, "is so evasive today that fundamentalists looking at all the schlock going on under the rubric of theology cut through it with the simplest and bluntest of instruments—namely, the inerrancy of the Bible. It is simple, blunt, and I think totally inadequate. Nonetheless, one can understand, because, damn it, you need something to cut through it. Here is where they decide whether you are with them or against them." On the other hand, if there is no submission to external authority, then no difference will be made—theologically, ecclesiastically, or otherwise—Neuhaus noted.

Campbell responded stirringly to Wright's question. "If I really thought it didn't make any difference, I sure would get out of the church and out of the work that I am doing. I understand my vocation as training men and women for Christian ministry to be engaged in a project that has ultimate significance. I really believe that. And I really believe that it makes a difference that people come into and live in Christian community. If I didn't, I'd get out of it. I think the question is the right one, and how we answer it is decisive. I think the difference between the early Methodists and latter-day Methodists is that those early circuit riders in America really believed that what they did every day made a difference."

Neuhaus then ventured another answer to Wright's question: "Even if there were no empirically demonstrable difference made, still this Word is to be spoken, these sacraments are to be done, and this life is to be lived—because it is true. We are damned eternally if we don't speak this Word and do these sacraments and live this life. Unless that is the foundation of it all, the jig is up."

With that the participants prepared to take on the last topic of conference—orthodoxy with a "neo" attached.

Neo-Orthodoxy, Again

As Elliott Wright had set the terms of the second to the last part of the conference discussion, Robert Lynn of the Lilly Endowment set the terms for the last part of the discussion. Lynn's concern was neo-orthodoxy: "So much of the form and character of Oden's argument is in the form of a jeremiad. That is a very powerful literary form. I am often reminded by friends of my proclivity for jeremiad. At this point, though, I want to be cautious. I remember Edwin Lewis, who wrote *Christian Manifesto*, which I happened to read at the end of

World War II. I was deeply troubled about Christian faith then, and my Calvinist pastor pulled that book off his shelf for me. In his own way, Edwin Lewis at Drew Theological School in the 1930s and 1940s acted as a precursor of neo-orthodoxy. I think we have to ask what happened to neo-orthodoxy the last time around. Do we know enough about our history to engage in jeremiad? Those are questions, not just rhetorical statements."

Cooper, who tends to equate neo-orthodoxy and Reinhold Niebuhr, was surprised that Lynn seemed to be implying that neo-orthodoxy had failed. "The Niebuhrian project was dropped by the generation of his students and has today been restarted by the next theological generation. But by no means did it fail in Niebuhr's own time. It could not simply be reiterated in ours. But it certainly is a viable model today, from my point of view."

Neuhaus joined Cooper in his optimism, although he was a bit more tentative. "Historically, the passage of neo-orthodoxy has something to say, and its apparent decline is a part of the current situation that we have to come to terms with. In terms of beginning again, take Jim Reichley's book *Religion in American Public Life*—its reception and the argument about the relationship between republican virtue, religious presuppositions, and the American experiment. Some people, no offense intended, would say that that is not very new. But the fact that it has gained the attention it has might just suggest that we have been through a thirty- or forty-year fit of absentmindedness, especially in higher education and among the new class, the culture-defining elite of our society, with regard to what was once elementary. Hasn't the new beginning already happened? Juices are flowing far beyond this room. People are rediscovering what at one time was self-evident. But it is no longer simply a rediscovery, because it comes after we have seen the consequences of the prolonged fit of absentmindedness—the consequences religiously, politically, culturally, and otherwise. So isn't the new beginning already underway?"

Dennis Campbell, for one, said, "It is."

Lynn added, "I hope it is. I hope that it will be accompanied in the early stages by extraordinarily disciplined intellectual work. One reason neo-orthodoxy ran into theological problems was that it handled too easily and too simply the problems of paradox and truth. I'm not saying we should try to slow down this cycle; I'm saying we should face the fact that we are in for some very long, disciplined years of historical work in finding how we got to the present place."

At this point Cooper noted a Niebuhrian irony. Niebuhr, he

claimed, just wanted to help create a more self-critical liberalism. While Niebuhr's students dropped that ball, today's neo-conservatives are ready and willing to pick it up. But isn't the word "neo-conservative" really a misnomer, inquired Neuhaus. Of course, replied Cooper.

"Why did Edwin Lewis not work?" Oden asked in his summary statement. "The answer, of course, is that Edwin Lewis did work. I would not be here were it not for Edwin Lewis. Why didn't the Niebuhrs and Albert Outler and Will Herberg work? Well, of course, they did work. Many of us would not be around this table if it weren't for Reinhold, H. Richard, Albert, and Will. So neo-orthodoxy is still very much alive, and it is alive in us, but not uncritically.

"My problem with neo-orthodoxy is that it was never catholic enough. It was too Protestant. It never had an adequate ecclesiology. It never had a doctrine of ministry. You look for it in Reinhold Niebuhr, but you cannot find it.

"It may sound like I am angry," said Oden, "but there is a kind of love for the church that requires anger, that requires confrontation. Anger is always endangered by excess and pride. But we are at a point where we need to learn to say No more clearly than we have learned. About this Protestant smile—we all know too well how to smile it."

Then Oden concluded his portion of the conference and the entire conference as well. "I certainly and wholeheartedly join Robert Lynn in hoping for solid theological work. But knowledge will not get us where we want to go. Knowledge alone will not get us where we want to go. That is an Enlightenment illusion that we should have acknowledged a long time ago."

The conference ended without a solid consensus on where the believable future of American Protestantism indeed lies. On this issue, the most fundamental of the conference, no votes were taken. And, contrary to a tongue-in-cheek suggestion of one of the participants, no bets were placed on it.

Despite the absence of an clear consensus about where the future of American Protestantism lies, however, there did appear to be some agreement about where it does not lie. It does not seem to lie in the present work of the mainline denominations, for instance—particularly, in their church-and-society and global-ministries offices. Nor does it seem to lie in the programs of those who are pitted in the Kulturkampf against the denominational officers of the new class or in the programs of the Religious New Right. Basically, it does not seem likely that the future lies in any of the present and prevailing options within American Protestantism.

If Tom Oden is right, the future, if it is to be promising and perhaps even hold a New Reformation, will entail more than a new Protestant scholasticism. All kinds of knowledge—theological, historical, sociological, political, and so on—will of course be important to that future. But knowledge alone will not be sufficient. And granted, a new orthodoxy, a neoorthodoxy, will be a necessary component of a reformed Protestantism. But even if a new neo-orthodoxy were to take the nature and mission of the church seriously (which the neo-orthodoxy of Reinhold Niebuhr tended not to do), it would not be enough to bring about the reformation of American Protestantism. That, says Oden, would require divine effort and intervention—specifically, the effort and intervention of the Holy Spirit.

That confession is, on the one hand, an occasion for a profound pessimism, for it underscores the almost irredeemable fix into which American Protestantism—and particularly the mainline—has worked itself. On the other hand, it provides an occasion for deep optimism—or at least trust—in the faithful and mysterious providence of God over his church and his world, even over the American Protestant churches and American society.

Reform came to the church while Martin Luther and friends sat at table and drank their beer, or so Luther claimed. The Word, he said, did all the work of reforming the church; he claimed no credit for himself. That is surely not the whole story of the Reformation, but it is an important part of the story. If there is to be a New Reformation or even a new orthodoxy in American Protestantism, that aspect of the first Reformation will undoubtedly be repeated.

For Further Investigation

The following books, chapters, and articles on American Protestantism are written or suggested by conference participants.

Ahlstrom, Sidney E. *A Religious History of the American People*. New Haven: Yale University Press, 1972.

Ammerman, Nancy T. *Bible Believers: Fundamentalists in the Modern World*. New Brunswick, N.J.: Rutgers University Press, 1987.

Bellah, Robert N. *The Broken Covenant: American Civil Religion in a Time of Trial*. New York: Seabury, 1975.

_____. "Civil Religion in America." *Daedalus* 96 (Winter 1967): 1-21.

_____. *Habits of the Heart*. San Francisco: Harper & Row, 1986.

Campbell, Dennis M. *Authority and the Renewal of American Theology*. New York: Pilgrim Press, 1976.

Cooper, John W. *The Theology of Freedom: The Legacy of Jacques Maritain and Reinhold Niebuhr*. Macon: Mercer University Press, 1985.

Derr, Thomas Sieger, John W. Baker, and A. E. Dick Howard. *Church, State, and Politics*. Washington: American Trial Lawyers Foundation, 1981.

Dobson, Edward. *Fundamentalist Phenomenon*. Garden City, N.Y.: Doubleday, 1980.

_____. *In Search of Unity*. Nashville: Thomas Nelson, 1985.

Gaustad, Edwin. *Dissent in American Religion*. Chicago: University of Chicago Press, 1973.

Hadden, Jeffrey K. *The Gathering Storm in the Churches*. Garden City, N.Y.: Doubleday, 1970.

Hadden, Jeffrey K., and Charles E. Swann, *Prime Time Preachers*. Reading, Mass.: Addison-Wesley, 1981.

Handy, Robert T. *A Christian America: Protestant Hopes and Historical Realities*. 2d ed. New York: Oxford University Press, 1984.

Hutcheson, Richard G., Jr. *Mainline Churches and the Evangelicals*. Atlanta: John Knox Press, 1981.

Kelley, Dean M. *Why Conservative Churches Are Growing*. 1972; Macon: Mercer University Press, 1986.

Lynn, Robert W., and Elliott Wright, *The Big Little School: Two Hundred Years of the Sunday School.* 2d ed. Nashville: Abingdon Press, 1980.

Marsden, George, ed. *Evangelicalism and Modern America.* Grand Rapids: Eerdmans, 1984.

Neuhaus, Richard John. *The Naked Public Square.* Grand Rapids: Eerdmans, 1984.

Niebuhr, H. Richard. *Christ and Culture.* New York: Harper & Row, 1951.

_____. *The Kingdom of God in America.* 1937; New York: Harper & Row, 1959.

Novak, David. *Christianity in Jewish Eyes.* New York: Oxford University Press, 1988.

_____. *The Image of the Non-Jew in Judaism.* Lewiston: Edwin Mellen Press, 1983.

Ramsey, Paul. *Who Speaks for the Church?* Nashville: Abingdon, 1967.

Reichley, A. James. *Religion in American Public Life.* Washington: Brookings Institution, 1985.

Roof, Wade Clark, and William McKinney. *American Mainline Religion: Its Changing Shape and Future.* New Brunswick, N.J.: Rutgers University Press, 1987.

Roof, Wade Clark, and Robert S. Michaelsen, eds. *Liberal Protestantism: Realities and Possibilities.* New York: Pilgrim Press, 1986.

Silk, Mark. *Spiritual Politics: Religion and America since World War II.* New York: Simon & Schuster, 1988.

Smith, Timothy L. *Revivalism and Social Reform: American Protestantism on the Eve of the Civil War.* 1957; Gloucester, Mass.: Peter Smith, 1976.

Tocqueville, Alexis de, *Democracy in America.*

Turner, James. *Without God, Without Creed: The Origins of Unbelief in America.* Baltimore: The Johns Hopkins University Press, 1985.

Willimon, William H. "Christianity and the Fox Theater." *Christian Century,* October 22, 1986, pp. 914-16.

_____. *What's Right with the Church.* San Francisco: Harper & Row, 1985.

Wilson, John F. *Public Religion in American Culture.* Philadelphia: Temple University Press, 1981.

Participants

Nancy T. Ammerman
Candler School of Theology
Emory University

Peter L. Berger
Boston University

Dennis M. Campbell
The Divinity School
Duke University

John W. Cooper
Ethics and Public Policy Center

Dean C. Curry
Department of History and
    Political Science
Messiah College

Thomas Sieger Derr
Department of Religion
Smith College

Edward G. Dobson
Fundamentalist Journal

Anne T. Fraker
Center for American Studies
Indiana University - Purdue
    University at Indianapolis

Jeffrey K. Hadden
Department of Sociology
University of Virginia

Milton Himmelfarb
Formerly Editor of the *American
    Jewish Year Book*, Institute of
    Human Relations, and
    formerly Director of
    Information and Research
    Services, American Jewish
    Committee

James Davison Hunter
Department of Sociology
University of Virginia

Richard G. Hutcheson, Jr.
Senior Fellow
The Rockford Institute
Center on Religion & Society

Dean M. Kelley
National Council of Churches

Jean Caffey Lyles
The Lutheran

Robert Wood Lynn
Lilly Endowment, Inc.

Meg H. Madson
Office of the Presiding Bishop
The American Lutheran Church

George Marsden
The Divinity School
Duke University

153

Richard John Neuhaus
The Rockford Institute
Center on Religion & Society

David Novak
Jewish Theological Seminary of
    America

Thomas C. Oden
Theological School
Drew University

A. James Reichley
The Brookings Institution

Wade Clark Roof
Department of Sociology
University of Massachusetts

Mark Silk
Author
Milton, MA

Timothy L. Smith
Department of History
    Johns Hopkins University

Paul T. Stallsworth
The Rockford Institute
Center on Religion & Society

James Turner
Department of History
University of Michigan

George S. Weigel, Jr.
The James Madison Foundation

William H. Willimon
Duke University Chapel

John F. Wilson
Project on Church and State
Princeton University

Elliott Wright
National Conference of
    Christians and Jews